# TRINIDAD
## My Home—My People
### Life and service of EDITH JOHNSON

Man Stifter
Blessings!

Edith Johnson

# TRINIDAD

## My Home—My People

### Life and service of **EDITH JOHNSON**

Edith Johnson shares her 54-years of testings and triumphs
in helping build authentic followers of Jesus
in Trinidad, West Indies.

**As told to**
# Max Inglis

TRINIDAD MY HOME—MY PEOPLE
By: MAX INGLIS
Copyright © 2008
GOSPEL FOLIO PRESS
All Rights Reserved

Published by
GOSPEL FOLIO PRESS
304 Killaly St. W.
Port Colborne, ON L3K 6A6
CANADA

ISBN: 9781897117958

Cover design by Rachel Brooks

All Scripture quotations from the
King James Version unless otherwise noted.

Printed in USA

# Contents

Forward.................................................................................7
Preface.................................................................................9
With Deep Gratitude...........................................................11
1  Going Back to My Roots..........................................13
2  Family, Faith and Fears............................................19
3  I'm Going to be a Missionary....................................21
4  Season of Despair....................................................27
5  Preparing for that Great Adventure.........................33
6  Hello Trinidad.........................................................37
7  First Fruits..............................................................41
8  Michael, Young Disciple.........................................47
9  A Dream Comes True...............................................51
10 Teamwork......................................................................55
11 Fresh Footprints............................................................59
12 Miracles in Marabella ...................................................63
13 A Real Fish Story...........................................................69
14 Lady with the Broad-brimmed Hat................................73
15 Do Angels Use Telephones?..........................................77
16 Camping: Growth of a Vision........................................81
17 Ridgewalk Camp Becomes a Reality..............................85
18 Friends, Coffee and a Bible Study.................................91
19 Mischievous Memories..................................................97
20 Furnished and Free........................................................99
21 Vicious Attack..............................................................103
22 Three Intercessors .......................................................107
23 Lord, Teach Me to Pray................................................111
24 Advancing: Three More Villages Open their Doors........115
Epilogue............................................................................119
Appendix A:  What is World Team?............................121
Appendix B:  What is the ECWI? ...............................124
Appendix C:  Snapshot of Trinidad & Tobago ...........126

Edith

# FORWARD

I am honored to have the privilege of writing this Forward to introduce you to the life story of one of God's choice servants, Edith Johnson.

Edith has been a special friend for over forty years. Stephen and I first met her when we arrived in Trinidad in the 1960s for a week-long Keswick meeting. Those days were days of precious fellowship, prayer, and sharing with the Christians in that area. It was obvious to us that Edith was respected and loved.

It is always amazing to me how quickly and easily relationships are made when the Lord is in the lives of those we meet along life's way. A motto on one of Edith's bookmarkers is John 12:24, *"Except a corn of wheat fall into the ground and die, it abideth alone."* This death-life makes all the difference in whether the Lord is over all aspects of our lives or whether we are in control of our "self-life."

When I presented my life to the Lord, I was seventeen and it was Romans 12:1-2 that broke me, *"I beseech you therefore, brethren, by the mercies of God, that you present your bodies a living sacrifice, holy, acceptable to God, which is your reasonable service. And do not be conformed to this world, but be transformed by the renewing of your mind, that you may prove what is that good and acceptable and perfect will of God."*—I wanted to be a "living sacrifice." Edith knew, and continues to know, that death to self. It has been the mark of the life you are going to read about in this book, *TRINIDAD My Home—My People.*

Edith's love of sports and activity has made her a mover and shaker! I like that because, together with Stephen, my husband, our heart's desire was to keep up with God and His plans, and that meant availability and adaptability. That's how Edith did ministry. Wherever and whenever the door was open she went in and took the opportunity, even if she really had something else she felt she was more suited in doing. God's plan was best.

Edith became fearless. Through a horrible experience that would have broken another person's faith and trust, she learned to lean completely on the One who has said, *"I will never leave you nor forsake you"* (Heb. 13:5). It would have been easy and understandable if after the physical attack Edith endured, she had decided to go home. Many have gone home for lesser reasons. That's why my heart and mind have been drawn to Luke 9:62, *"No man, having put his hand to the plough, and looking back, is fit for the kingdom of God."* "Looking back" or "turning back" are powerful phrases that have no place in the life of this faithful servant, Edith Johnson.

I pray that this book will bless and challenge all who read it. God will use anyone who decides to follow Jesus, no looking back.

Heather Olford,
Memphis, Tennessee

# PREFACE

Every so often you come across a person who has not only dreamed a seemingly unattainable dream, but against all odds is living it out. Such is Edith Johnson.

The dictionary meaning of "trek" suits Edith to a T because trek or trekking carries the thought of a "difficult" or "arduous" journey. What Edith did her first years in Trinidad, walking everywhere in the heat of the tropics, easily conveys her rugged determination.

I first met Edith in western Pennsylvania, at our West Indies Mission headquarters. The second time we met she was on site reaching out to the people of Trinidad in the Caribbean. As a reporter for our Mission magazine, *Harvest Today*, I had the privilege of visiting several churches in Trinidad whose people allowed their lives to shine like beacon lights.

Many times in listening to snatches of her life story, I picked up the makings of a fascinating biography. As a young child, Edith dreamed of one day telling children in Africa about Jesus' love. Later, after being rejected three times by mission agencies serving in Africa, she eventually ended up in the West Indies. Little did she realize in her early years, she would be asked to do something she felt no woman should have to do.

In his book *"Drumbeats that Changed the World,"* author Joseph F. Conley gives tribute to this missionary in Trinidad when he wrote:

> "For Men Only. That is what Edith Johnson thought in 1966 when asked to take over a start-up work in Arima, Trinidad.

'This is a man's job,' she argued with West Indies Mission leadership. Johnson's comfort zone was working with women and children—not planting churches."

"There was no man around," Edith said back then, "so I and my colleague went to work and we ended up planting four churches." Later, Edith teamed with younger missionaries in church plants and other worthy projects that today stretch over the island nation of Trinidad and Tobago.

I have known Edith for 54 years. She is a remarkable woman. Many a time she has left my wife and me in the dust as we tried walking with her. She is always looking into the future with visionary plans for the churches in her islands.

When she asked me whether I would be willing to write and publish her life story, I told her, "Edith, I have never published a book and at my age, taking up such a task could be hazardous to my health." Edith's persistence prevailed.

All I can say is enjoy the journey. May her faith, her trust, her persevering trek with never a thought of turning back, rub off on you as it has done on hundreds of others.

Maxton Inglis
Former Editor, World Team

# WITH DEEP GRATITUDE

What a wonderfully active crew we had in launching *TRIN-IDAD My Home — My People*. We also want to thank you who carried a burden of prayer for this venture. You were the many behind the scenes who prayed the book into existence, right to its finish.

Nalini Victor — dear friend from India, your assistance in the first chapters was valuable.

Margaret Keeler — what would we have done without your faithful prodding, and husband Richard — working for hours on cassette tapes. You two are a gracious gift.

Ruby Thompson — faithful prayer partner, your support over 35 years is priceless.

David Ford — when the book almost died, you became a strong encourager.

Peter and Kay Harris — you opened your home for the team making cassettes. Cheers!

Paul and Evelyn Kratz — your patience and hours of computer expertise, photo work and chauffeuring were such a boost!

Helen Johnston — you and your late husband, (my dear brother Earl) read and critiqued early chapters. Also, Christal Peters, you did likewise. We cannot forget your labors of love.

Dean & Edith Franklin and Duane Moyer — you were our team of encouragers. Thanks for your critique of the early manuscripts.

Donna Williamson—faithful 17-year team mate, your hospitality, ideas on manuscript and choosing photos for the book, were tasks well done.

Jim Griffiths—computer assistant and technical engineer to my author—your part will not soon be forgotten. Your wife Ann's helpful hints and ideas on publishing were fitting.

Our publisher—Sam Cairns and crew at GOSPEL FOLIO PRESS, Port Colborne, Ontario, did a masterful job in preparing manuscript, editing, and producing a very presentable product.

May all of you who had a part in *TRINIDAD My Home— My People* share, now and eternally, in the rewards from my humble story.

—E. Johnson.

# 1
# Going Back to My Roots

I woke up with a start. I had been sleeping in my duplex on the expansive gated property of the Texaco Oil Company in Trinidad, West Indies. A male intruder was shouting out his evil intentions, "I'm going to rape you! I'm going to rape you." I tried desperately to fight him off. It was 3:30 a.m. but no one seemed to hear my cries for help.

My childhood dreams did not include this kind of struggle. Back then, and alone in the woods, I envisioned the day when I would take my little New Testament and tell dark-skinned boys and girls overseas about Jesus. I certainly never envisioned having to fight for my very life...

\*\*\* \*\*\* \*\*\*

But first I really want to take you on a trip back to my childhood. So come with me as we visit Preston, a village in western Washington. Thirty miles east of Seattle, just off Interstate 90, Preston is one of those beautiful forested villages all but hidden from view of travelers zipping by. Each year Old Man Winter drapes his white mantle over the surrounding Cascade Mountains.

At the beginning of the nineteenth century this village came into being mainly through an influx of Swedish immigrants. Prominent at the edge of town in early years was the smokestack of Preston's one sawmill, the main source of employment for the men of the district. Also in the early years the little Baptist Church poked its spire above homes that were nestled nearby. Built in the year 1900, this place of worship remains as the only church in Preston.

Respected and known by most of the community, my father, Ronald Johnson, was foreman of the mill and along with my hard-working mother, Mabel, they made a formidable team. My dad, with his handsome face and tall frame, was not only a man's man, he had a wonderfully gentle nature and knew how to work. Mom was a devoted wife and homemaker, known for her Swedish breads and rolls. Dad always had a garden and Mom canned much of what he grew. Solid testimony was attributed by the townspeople to the faith of both Mom and Dad. One of the mill workers declared, "There is only one man who can talk to me about being a Christian. That man is Ronald Johnson because he lives what he preaches." At Mom's funeral several people voiced similar sentiments concerning mother's simple trust in the Lord.

After three girls blessed the Johnson home, Dad prayed, "Heavenly Father, please grant this next little one to be a son to grow up with our three daughters." The parents were a wee bit disappointed when I, the fourth member arrived that 25th day of August in 1928, but very quickly that disappointment was replaced with love and joy over this very active addition. Dad insisted that the new baby bear her mother's name. Together they felt she should be called Edith Mabel. "Just maybe she might be our missionary," they agreed. Little did they realize their fifth one would be a son and Earl would become the preacher of the family. So the Johnson roll call eventually numbered six children: Marjorie, June, Lois, Edith, Earl and Roger.

Growing up in Preston where people in the village knew each other, where doors didn't get locked at night, and where many of the Scandinavian population spoke little English, there was a real sense of community—they all took part in raising us children. After supper the kids played on the street and were called in at dusk.

One of the things I remember about my growing up years

was life outdoors: swinging on vine maples and climbing tall trees like the fir growing close to our home. In fact, the challenge was that the one who dared tie the ribbon the highest was the winner. I would proudly tie my ribbon on the highest branch possible, then invite my mother outside to view the ribbon fluttering on high. This brought a gasp from my Mom. "Yah, you von't be doing that too often, Edie." Out of necessity, my dear Mom had to be strict as well as protective of her flock. My philosophy of life was fairly naïve. Why would Mother call me in to do housework when I could have so much fun outside? I wasn't old enough to work in the house. Maybe when I reached my teens I'd help her with the housework, but certainly not now.

To show you how the community spirit prevailed in Preston, the parents planned a Halloween party for all the children. We Johnsons were allowed to go but with the provision that we come straight home and not get involved in any pranks. Temptation overcame my older sisters, and I confess that I wasn't about to be left out. The school windows were properly soaped and punishment followed the next day at school.

However, since I was too young to be involved in my sisters' discipline, the teacher whom I idolized, June Runbeck, made me stay at school and learn some poetry. I remember having to memorize the following lines while tears trickled down my face:

> "Animal crackers and cocoa to drink,
> This is the finest of suppers I think.
> When I grow up and can have what I please,
> I think I shall always insist upon these."

I would find myself sorely tempted when Dad would warn me specifically not to ride my borrowed bike across the snow-covered bridge that spanned Raging River near the church. I yielded and a bleeding knee cap resulted from a nasty spill. This seemed to me the reward for my disobedience. It happened a couple of days before the Christmas program where I was to perform. Instead of letting my disobedience smoulder, Mother lovingly made me a round patch to cover the knee. In a pageant five of us were to pin points of a star in place. Having to kneel on my bad knee, I mistakenly put my point in the wrong direction. All five of us broke out in uncontrollable giggles. Our teacher was rightfully annoyed and I was reprimanded by both teacher and parents.

I was only five when the great depression of the 1930s hit. Mom would do her best to make tasty meals. Still we would get tired of the same old things and often we'd whine about our simple fare, that is until Dad would get up from the table, go over to the wood box and choose a kindling stick. Then he would come back and lay the stick on the table. The complaining stopped immediately. I never remember him having to use the stick on us. Sometimes we would sneak some of the icing off our piece of cake and lay it almost out of sight. That would make wonderful candy as we went out to play—so I thought. Dad caught on and cured us by coming over to the table, locating the piece of icing and popping it into his mouth. We didn't try that again.

Dad loved to take us fishing. One time we had a cabin lined up, so we thought, and arrived to find it wasn't available. Not being discouraged, Dad threw down a tarp on the ground and the sixteen of us slept side by side under the stars.

Another time he took us fishing in the ocean near Puget Sound. My brother and I decided we would walk out to some rocks off shore and fish from there. What we didn't know was that the tide was coming in. Only Mother was on shore. Dad had walked elsewhere and Mom could see what was happening to us. At the last moment she got our attention and called to us and watched closely as we waded to shore. Oh yes, there was also the time that Dad, Earl and I were in a rented boat and some fairly dense fog set in. Out of the mist loomed a huge ferry. Dad got us out of the way in a hurry. And I will never forget the time Dad had rented a boat and we were quite a distance from shore when the strong tide pulled us out to sea. That wouldn't have been so bad but we spotted some active whirlpools. Dad had the motor wide open and with the help of the oars and after one major struggle, got us to some bushes offshore. Dad told Earl and me to wade to the beach and follow the trail along the shore and we'd eventually meet up with Mother. He told us he couldn't leave the boat as it was rented and he'd try to get it back to where he got it. We did find Mom, but the wait for Dad brought us much anxiety as it took close to three hours for him to get back to his little family. We had visions of Dad being somehow swept out to sea. Thankfully that was not the case.

I will not soon forget the fateful day that our school bus collided with a big tanker. The tank split, spilling gas all over the road and all of us traipsed through the gas-soaked roadway to safety. I distinctly remember a service of thanksgiving held in the Preston Community Center, where the townspeople offered their thanks to God for sparing our lives. As youngsters we little realized what could have happened had a spark set off an explosion. Did God possibly have something special in mind for me when He spared my life? I often pondered that question.

Preston Baptist, my home church, celebrates its 100th anniversary.

# 2
# Family, Faith and Fears

Often I was reminded of the heritage which my God-fearing parents had imprinted on my life. From early childhood my heart had been tender toward the Lord. From the time we were infants, my folks had earnestly prayed that the Lord would be central in our lives. They reinforced this by being godly role models and by their willingness to serve Jesus in everyday practical living. Dad served as a deacon and Sunday School superintendent as well as teaching the adult class. My parents took us to church each week without fail. Then, right after lunch they loaded their tribe into the trusty Buick and drove the 30 miles to a village called Ravensville. There we were welcomed by a boisterous group of children eager to take part in their very own Sunday School. We'd make the trek back to Preston, only to eat and get ready for evening church. Often I'd ask whether I could play ball with the neighbor kids rather than go to church. But this was not an option.

Early in life I sensed the need of allowing the Lord Jesus to take charge of my life. When learning the Scriptures and being taught by excellent Sunday School teachers, I was often fearful of what the Bible taught about Jesus returning to earth to take His own away. I knew I was not ready. I remember rushing home from school on some of those days, hoping against hope my mother would not be missing. I was always relieved to discover her on her knees in the bedroom praying for her little flock. Other times she was sitting on her old stool behind the pantry door sipping a cup of coffee. A haunting fear of Jesus' return was one of the things that got me thinking seriously about God and whether I was not only ready, but also fit to meet Him.

You might say that my spiritual journey came to fruition at Lake Sammamish Bible Camp, not many miles from our home in Washington. That's where I knelt and asked God to forgive me of all those little sins that felt like a huge burden. Can you imagine the peace that now took the place of those desperate fears of being left behind? I was only nine at the time but I had no doubts about the assurance God gave me. Wow, I was now His very own child.

Shortly after this, Mom and Dad took me to a special afternoon conference meeting at Sammamish where the pastor emphasized the importance of giving our lives completely to Jesus. I wanted to do this so badly that I must have been wiggling. Mother caught the clue and asked, "Edith, do you want to go forward today?" Quickly I said, "Yes, I do." To this day I have no better memory than that of Mother taking hold of my hand and together walking down the aisle—it seemed like a mile long. We knelt and I told God I really wanted to be His servant.

Sometimes that vision dimmed, particularly when I got into high school. I was excited to be in the high school activities, especially since they had a super gymnastics program. Football and baseball with the guys used up much of my energy. The summer I graduated from high school, the yearbook carried the statement, "Edith Johnson is the best all around athlete this school has ever had." What was not stated was that my parents groaned at the pairs of shoes they had to buy for their superactive daughter—a brand new pair every month. It was at this juncture that I became so passionate about a possible career in sports that I remember reasoning with God: "Lord, I can serve You as a physical education teacher. I can tell these kids about You." My early thoughts of going overseas to teach boys and girls about Jesus also faded. It took a missionary, Rhodie Olson, to change all that.

# 3
# I'm Going to be a Missionary

Rhodie Olson had started for Africa in Spring 1941, but the ship she was on, the *Zamzam*, was torpedoed during World War II. God spared her life. When she visited Preston, her mother's home area, she spoke at our church. I will never forget what Rhodie said one night at youth group. "I do not believe God brought me back home just to see my parents before I go to Africa. I believe with all my heart He brought me home just to speak to you young people tonight." She went on to say, "You know you can go any place in the world today and you will find that Singer Sewing Machines are there; that is true of Coca Cola as well. But there are many, many places where the Gospel has never gone." In my heart the Lord was saying, "I want you to go to a specific place that I will show you." I thought, "I've got to get out of here."

On my way out I didn't want my peers to see me crying, so I dashed past them and actually walked up to Rhodie and said, "God wants me to be a missionary, but I don't want to." She was very wise and invited me to sit down and talk. After we chatted awhile, she said something I have never forgotten. "Edith, if God could make you willing to be a missionary, would you be willing to let Him do that?" I realized that once I agreed, I would not have an argument with God. Then she said, "Let's get down on our knees and you tell God that you will be willing to be made willing." So I knelt and told the Lord that, and He flooded my heart with peace. As soon as I said, "Lord, I will be a missionary," my whole outlook changed. Now I was really excited that one day I would go out as one of God's messengers.

My folks were willing to get me started in further training and after two trial years in two different places, one a secular college and the other a Bible school, I knew God didn't want me in either. It was through the very warm-hearted student leaders, that each year served at Sammamish Bible Camp, that I became interested in attending Prairie Bible Institute in Alberta, Canada. But I was sure that I could never go there because of the strict rules. I had heard that the boys could not talk to the girls and that student girls must let their hair grow to a certain length. It all seemed so foolish to me. I should probably look at other schools.

One day, when Principal L.E. Maxwell was speaking at our Bible conference, he asked me after one meeting, "Are you thinking of coming to Prairie?" I didn't want to answer because I knew I didn't want to go. I found that I was really trying to run away from God. Mercifully, the Lord kept after me. I ended up at Prairie along with my brother, Earl. As children, Earl and I were not only next to one another in age, we had played together as youngsters and grew up with similar goals of reaching lost people. Earl trained to be a pastor, and with his wife, Helen, served several churches until God took him home a few years ago.

My four years at Prairie were unforgettable—for the *"corn of wheat"* principle began living out in my life. I saw it happening in the older students as well as in the lives of the staff. If a kernel of wheat is going to reproduce, it must go through the death process. This truth challenged me to the depths.

In my early days of summer work at Prairie, one of the first rules I broke (no running in the dormitories) happened when the slipper I was wearing hit a warped floor board and drove a long sliver into my foot. I ended up in the infirmary for several days. While there the Lord let me think through my sin of disobedience. I was told, "You're going to be assigned to clean slop buckets." I knew that all those who had to do this hated the assignment. I was sure at first I'd not like it one bit either. There was no running water except in the bathrooms, so we all had a slop bucket in our rooms. But the men's buckets were harder to clean because of the crust of shaving cream around the inside of the bucket. Day after day, this job actually ended up giving me the joy that I never dreamt possible. I did it for the Lord, maybe that was the answer. I thank God that this *"corn of wheat"* principle was becoming ingrained in me before entering any Christian service.

Every spring at Prairie Bible Institute, recruits from different home missions would share their needs in chapel service. These were potential missionaries who appealed to us to venture into the out-of-the-way places that had little gospel light. The rewards, not always stated, were promised as eternal with little likelihood of payment in this life, and with living conditions rustic at best.

A Prairie Bible student from Calgary, Alberta, Muriel Hayne (now with the Lord) and I were assigned to work in a remote area in northern BC. Rolla was near Mile 0 of the Alaska Highway, under the Ministry of the CSSM (Canadian Sunday School Mission). It was not uncommon to have the temperatures drop to 50 below zero at nights and 35 below during the day. And then there was the fun of producing drinking water. We had a 50-gallon drum sitting close to our kitchen stove that we filled with snow. That became our source of water for every need. In daylight hours everything stayed frozen. We found ourselves digging chunks of frozen wood out of the ground and chopping them up in order to keep our fire going. In summer we carried on some well-attended Vacation Bible Schools with children that knew nothing about the Scriptures. Often our pay was the food that neighbors brought us. One woman provided simple fare on weekdays. This was really the life. I guess God knew best the training we needed before going overseas.

\* \* \*

I also discovered some things about cars and how they work. Where do you pour the oil when the dipstick shows nearly empty? Well, when all else fails, you pour it down the dipstick hole! When two of my male friends found me doing this, they roared with laughter. But they were kind enough to show me the oil cap.

Another time, driving up BC's Fraser Canyon, I was trying my hardest to meet a deadline. (There were plenty of those in my life.) I left Surrey early one morning hoping to get to Williams Lake by 4:00 p.m. the same evening. I was hoping that I wouldn't have to drive any of those miles at night. Dad had checked my car carefully before I left, and as a last-minute decision, purchased a set of tire chains in case of snow. It did begin to snow and I grew alarmed at those snowflakes piling up. When I knew I wouldn't make it over the mountain without chains, I got out and tried to get those pesky chains on. "Help me, Lord, I'm scared and don't know how to do this, " I cried. Little did I realize with the onset of darkness, where I had gotten stuck, I was just a few feet from what would have been a straight drop to a gorge hundreds of feet below. I was so glad when a man driving a pick-up pulled up behind me. "Lady, whatever are you trying to do?" he asked. "Don't you know that not even men dare travel this road at night. Are you crazy?"

After he heard my need of meeting a deadline, he told me to follow him. Slipping in the fresh snow, our two vehicles made it to a garage in Boston Bar. A kind mechanic got the chains installed, but only after a major battle.

God had equipped me with a good measure of grit and determination. When I made up my mind to do something, I never looked back. It often carried me through many a test and many a mile. One of those tests came when I applied for missionary service.

At Bible school I had attended a prayer group that focused on Africa. I filled out my first application papers to a mission that worked in Africa. Between my third and fourth years at school, I had come down with rheumatic fever which left me with a heart murmur. I opened the reply to my first application and was jolted to read: "We do not feel that your health will stand up to the rigors of life in a field such as Africa." This was rejection slip number one. So I applied to a second mission with the same response. The third application came back with news every bit as discouraging. Oh, how I hurt inside! I prayed, "Heavenly Father, I believed with all my heart that I was to be a missionary to Africa but no one wants me. You will have to show me what to do now. I'm not going to fill out any more papers. Please will You show me where I am to go?"

Meet the family: (left to right)
Earl, Marj, June, Mom, Roger, Dad, Lois & yours truly (mid 1950s).

# 4
# Season of Despair

Before I continue on my journey, I need to retrace some steps. But it's important that I invite you to come with me. You see, I would be remiss if I didn't let you in on a very crucial season of my growth as a Christian. I even feel that if I didn't share this experience, you would never fully understand how necessary the lesson would have been for my future life and ministry. Do you remember how Jacob of old wrestled with a man all night until daybreak, demanding that he would not release him until something very significant happened? Genesis 32 tell us, *"Then He blessed him there."* Jacob declared he had seen God face to face. In another verse it said that the man told Jacob that *"You have struggled with God and man and have overcome."* This glimpse of Jacob's battle is not unlike what I went through.

In the spring of 1953, my four years at Prairie Bible Institute were history. Not only were those years of rich learning, I was able to watch the godly lives of those who taught and saw the changes in my fellow students. Far more times than I could recall I had listened to "the crucified life" that principal L.E. Maxwell had talked about. Teachers and students had modeled that life before me. I knew I didn't have what they had and deeply longed for the victorious life they exemplified! Was that never to be?

Also, during those college years, there was a distinct period when God revealed to me the utter sinfulness of my own heart. I found myself identifying with the Bride that Solomon had written about in his Song, how she cried out in the presence of her Lover about her darkness, *"Tell me, O thou whom my soul loveth, where thou feedest, where thou makest thy flock to rest at noon* (1:7). *My beloved spoke, and said unto me, Rise up, my love, my fair one, and come away"* (2:10). *"I sought him, but I found him not"* (3:1). *"I will seek him whom my soul loveth..."*(3:2).

I knew the Lord loved me, but I was not overwhelmed by that fact, mostly because I needed a closer more intimate walk with Jesus. I wanted to sense and know that love to the depths of my soul. Many a time I had called out to God for the abundant life that Jesus spoke about but He seemed so far away. Was my life pattern to be always one of ups and downs? Would my daily walk with Him just be spinning my wheels?

That summer of 1953 I was at home with my parents when I felt I had come to the end of my mediocre existence. I decided that without delay I would shut myself into my room and not come out until God had done His work in me. My parents were willing to go along with my plan, but I know that they probably didn't catch the full significance of my fasting. Mom would want to give me food or snacks to keep my energy up. But they were willing to give me the liberty that I needed at the time.

After an extended time in prayer and in the Scriptures, I did not know what I should do next. I paced the floor. Unexpectedly I came across a little booklet that I had acquired years earlier. God had used a small woman by the name of Aletta N. Jacobsz who had gone to Korea on a holiday. As an instrument in the Lord's hand, she had sparked a revival in a group of missionaries serving in Korea. I read through the little booklet and decided to follow the same steps she had used with those Korean missionaries.

First, Miss Jacobsz urged God's servants to get alone with Him. Then she introduced her readers to an outline arranged under five headings:

1. God's picture of the human heart
2. Some of God's standards
3. What my sin cost God

4. Sorrow for sin.

5. The life God promised and paid for on Calvary.

As I looked at the headings, I realized that with all my heart I wanted the life God promised and paid for on Calvary. My mind had been made up and with the Lord's enabling I would not settle for less.

I then did as Miss Jacobz had done. With my Bible open and a clean piece of paper, I asked the Lord to show me anything in my life that was hindering me from knowing this abundant life.

I began to go through the Scripture passages that she suggested and began to make a list of sins, shortcomings, failures and impurities as revealed by the Holy Spirit. With complete honesty, I considered the following verses:

## 1. God's picture of the human heart and His names for the sins that spring from it.

Galatians 5:19-21 (NIV) — *"The acts of the sinful nature are obvious: sexual immorality,"* (Well that one at least hasn't affected me. But then God's voice seemed to be reminding me of the verse that says *"As a man thinketh in his heart, so is he"*). O God, am I really guilty?

Galatians 5:19 again — *"impurity and debauchery"* (A few things came to mind; hesitantly I wrote them down); *"idolatry and witchcraft, hatred"* (Well, I really didn't hate that person, but I did avoid her every chance I got. O Lord, you mean….); *"discord, jealousy"* (now that's one I should put down, but at the time I don't know of a situation, unless…); *"fits of rage, selfish ambition"* (I do admit selfish ambition sometimes gets me…wow, do these verses ever picture my humanness); *"dissensions, factions and envy."* ("Jot that last one down, Edith," I seemed to hear the Spirit tell me); *"drunkenness, orgies, and the like"* (Father, I trust I am not guilty here.); I was beginning to get a glimpse of the real Edith, and here I was only finished with one verse.

Jeremiah 17:9 — *"The heart is deceitful above all things and desperately wicked."* (Lord, I'm so guilty). I wrote down "deceit." By now the tears were falling on my sheet of paper. I

29

had failed my Lord in so many areas, and I was going along without heartfelt sorrow.

Romans 8:5-8—*"Those who live according to the sinful nature have their minds set on what that nature desires"...* *"The sinful mind is hostile to God, it does not submit to God's law, nor can it do so. Those controlled by the sinful nature cannot please God."*

There were other verses like Mark 7:20-23, Colossians 3:5-9, James 3:2-8 and 2 Corinthians 7:1. As I dug out the sins that were named in these verses, you could almost hear my heart beating out that one word, "guilty." With horror I looked at what God was revealing to me. Then I began to look at some of God's standards.

## Some of God's STANDARDS

Matthew 5:41-44— *"If someone forces you to walk one mile, go with him two. Give to the one who asks you and do not turn away from the one who wants to borrow from you."*

1 Thessalonians 5:18— *"Give thanks in all circumstances, for this is God's will for you in Christ Jesus"* (Here I was, guilty as usual. How slow I was to give thanks, particularly when in the bad circumstances. I'm so sorry, Father.)

Malachi 3:10— *"Bring the whole tithe into the storehouse, that there may be food in my house. Test me in this, says the Lord Almighty, and see if I will not throw open the floodgates of heaven that you will not have room enough for it."*

1 Timothy 2:8-10— *"I want men everywhere to lift up holy hands in prayer, without anger or disputing. I also want women to dress modestly, with decency and propriety, not with braided hair or gold or pearls or expensive clothes, but with good deeds appropriate for women who profess to worship God."*

Other verses Miss Jacobsz listed were: Galatians 5:22, 26, I Peter 2:4, and Exodus 29:7.

Inwardly I was trembling as I faced the reality of my sinfulness. Why had I not been enjoying the abundant life that I so longed for? What I had seen as I looked at my life and what God had seen were so very different. God reminded me of unkind words that I had spoken, resentments that had been swept under the rug, plus a habit I had fallen into at work, using materials that belonged to my employer. Those were just a few of the things that the Holy Spirit brought to mind, stripping me of my self-righteousness.

With a broken heart and tears of bitterness, I promised the Lord that I would do what was required of me, confess my wrongdoings and make restitution where called for.

For about two days I lost interest in everything except getting right with God. All the steps that were pointed out had been taken, but I was still longing for something more.

In the little booklet that had become almost my constant companion, this dear servant, Alleta Jacobz, then suggested that you ask the Lord to reveal Himself to you in a new way and fill you with His Holy Spirit. I lost no time in making my response. With gladness I sensed I was clean and yielded. There alone by my bed I was given a vision of Calvary. It was as real as if I had been there when He was crucified. I do not know how long I stayed there, but I wept and wept at the foot of His cross. The knowledge in my head was now shifted to my heart. Galatians 2:20 became a reality in a new way. *"I have been crucified with Christ, and I no longer live, but Christ lives in me. The life I live in the body, I live by faith in the Son of God, who loved me and gave Himself for me."*

Gone now were the many struggles that I had experienced in my walk with the Lord.

My fresh encounter with the Son of God revolutionized my life. The Son had set me free. Pleasing Him became the motivation of my life. John 10:10, *"I have come that they might have life and that they might have it more abundantly."* My heart overflowed with joy. I now began to realize that I was indeed following in the train of His triumph. I knew that I would need to experience much more growth, but my Master's promise was sure when He said that I would be more than a conqueror. In a new way I could say, "Thank You, Lord, for Calvary!"

Thanks for being willing to experience my season of despair. I pray this helps you understand the journey that was now ahead for me. Here are two special stanzas from Amy Carmichael's familiar poem, "Make Me Thy Fuel":

From subtle love of softening things,
From easy choices, weakenings.
Not thus are spirits fortified,
Not this way went the Crucified.
From all that dims Thy Calvary,
O Lamb of God deliver me.

Give me the love that leads the way,
The faith that nothing can dismay,
The hope no disappointments tire,
The passion that will burn like fire.
Let me not sink to be a clod,
Make me Thy fuel, Flame of God

Can you imagine the peace that invaded my soul after years and years of struggle? I felt like a new person. I could face missionary life now with renewed zeal and expectancy from God. Hallelujah, what a Saviour!

# 5
# Preparing for that Great Adventure

The little magazine I happened to pick up was called *Whitened Harvest*. My eyes fell on a news article about my missionary friends Ben and Marguerite Penner. Working in the island of Trinidad in the south eastern Caribbean, Ben Penner was returning to Canada. He had been riding his bike in Trinidad with two of the field leader's boys on board when the bike struck a pothole. Three discs in Ben's back were injured, requiring surgery.

I wrote to the Mission, asking about Ben's injury and the Penners' ministry. The Harvest article had drawn attention to the need for personnel in Trinidad, with a plea for reinforcements. Jokingly I told the friend I was with, "I think I should go to Trinidad and help there." I didn't mean it any more than if I had told her I was going to the moon. I also casually asked some questions about West Indies Mission. Amazingly, in a few days a letter from the Mission arrived with a set of application papers for me to fill out. I had not asked for these. Having been turned down three times for Africa, I had little hope of getting to the West Indies. My friend encouraged me to fill out the papers. "It won't hurt," she added. As I struggled in prayer and before the Lord, I sensed that maybe the Lord was in this after all. The words kept repeating in my mind,

"Trinidad, Trinidad." I could not erase them. After the papers were filled out and sent in, I was invited to go to Candidate School. That was in August of 1955. And in doing so, a deep desire to become a person of faith began burning in my soul. Also, sparking this quest for the life of faith, I had been reading the biographies of Hudson Taylor, C.T. Studd, George Muëller, Isobel Kuhn and books written by Amy Carmichael. Reinforcing this desire to launch out into the life of faith were the role-models of my teachers at Prairie, my leaders at Lake Sammamish, and missionaries like Rhodie Olson.

I remember the day I arrived at our Mission's Headquarters near Homer City, PA. I was placed in the home of the Director, Elmer Thompson and his wife Evelyn. [1] To say that I was scared to death puts it mildly. But a month in their home gave me high respect for this humble and passionate couple. Besides attending candidate sessions, each incoming recruit was to do several hours of practical work. Allow me to say, I know how to wash windows, take care of walls that need cleaning and floors that need scrubbing.

After I was there for a time, Mr. Thompson, in his business-like manner, asked, "Miss Johnson, would you like to specify what field you are willing to go to, or would you be willing to go wherever the Mission sends you?"

Quickly I answered, "Yes, I'll go where the Mission sends me." I felt in my heart that he was going to say that you have been assigned to Trinidad. I was quite taken aback when I was told that after praying and waiting on God, the Board does not know where He would have you serve. He went on to say, "You go back home and when we know where the Lord would have you serve, we will write you."

Then one of the Board members started talking to me about gifts that missionaries need in going overseas. "Miss Johnson, it seems you have no gifts, you don't play the accordion, you don't sing …" Inwardly I was holding back, I felt crushed. To say this didn't hurt me was far from the truth. While I was trying to process what seemed to me one of the greatest blows in

---

1    See Appendix A for a short account of the founder, fields and ministry of World Team.

my life, I half heard the leader's next statement, "You go back home and when we know where the Lord would have you, we will write you." What a disappointment. Did this mean that I wouldn't be going to Trinidad? That I was totally lacking in all abilities to serve God? As I started out on that Greyhound bus across those hundreds of miles to Washington State, I was so thankful for my college years where I had been taught to go in crises like these. I also had time to review some of those words of the Apostle Paul to the Corinthian believers. In 1 Corinthians 1:28-29, *"He chose the lowly things of this world and the despised things — and the things that are not — to nullify the things that are, so that no one may boast before Him."* I sensed the Lord was healing my broken heart. I could once again trust Him for all that spiritual equiping I needed. (A number of years after this experience, I was told that the man who had counselled me as a candidate, told an old friend of mine, "Edith Johnson is one of the most effective missionaries we have in the Mission today").

Three weeks later, I looked at an envelope that had arrived from Mission headquarters and my hands trembled a little as I opened it and read, "After much prayer and waiting on God, we feel that the Lord wants you to serve in Trinidad." My heart burst out in praise to God. "Lord, I am to go to Trinidad and I'm excited. That's where I believed You would take me in the first place. Thank You for the affirmation. I can trust You."

Now with a sense of direction and with a new goal that I had never faced before, I took up the Mission's request that I trust God for $50 per month support. To raise my own support was a staggering thing for me.

As I was thinking of this task ahead of me, I had met a very missionary-minded pastor in Prince George, BC, Cliff Dietrich. I would phone him. God had used him to encourage me when he once wrote, "When you are accepted by your mission board, our church (the Evangelical Free Church) here wants to help you with your support." This was the beginning of a relationship that lasted nearly 60 years, until he passed away three years ago. This pastor (whom we lovingly called Pastor D) shared with me that not a day went by that he didn't pray for me. Then in addition to this church, my home church in Preston, WA, as well as the People's Church in Willowdale, ON, pledged some of my support. What a necessity and comfort to know that God's people were standing behind me in prayer as well as finance as I went overseas.

# 6
# Hello Trinidad

The downpour on our arrival at the airport in Trinidad soon disappeared. For the first time in my life I was looking at this beautiful island which Christopher Columbus had sighted on August 15th, 1498, his third voyage. What a tropical paradise! From its northwestern tip you can see Venezuela's coastline.

I feasted my eyes on real palm trees that I had previously seen only in pictures. I heard happy greetings exchanged as people passed one another.

But I will admit, as captivated as I was with the beauty of this Caribbean island, the most beautiful sight to me right then would have been a tall white man coming to my rescue. Harold Peters, one of the Mission's first arrivals in Trinidad, was nowhere to be seen. After a few awkward minutes trying to understand the accented English of the immigration officer, I walked into the waiting room. Now I would surely spot Mr. Peters. Not so.

Taxi drivers called, "Miss, may I give you a drop?" Each time I declined, feeling confident that missionary Peters would appear. Three hours passed and as the sun began to set, a friendly man posed a question. "Do you know where this Mr. Peters lives?" Yes, I told him, in Arouca. Then he kindly suggested we go to the police station there and inquire as to the Peters' residence. After we stopped at the station and asked if they knew of a Harold Peters, they told us, "Yes, he lives down this main road about half a mile." With the taxi driver's help, we ended up with bag and baggage at the Peters' home. To my dismay the Peters were not home. Would I panic or could I trust God? So I dragged my suitcases up and sat down on the front gallery (porch) of the Canadian couple's home.

What a strange world I looked out on as I sat alone on the porch. Thatched-roof houses with walls made of a strange mixture lined the street. Some of the homes were built of cement blocks with galvanized roofing. I was quite fascinated by a little man riding along in a cart pulled by a donkey. I soon discovered that bicycles were more common than cars. People with dark skin spoke with what seemed to me a heavy accent. As I waited for this Canadian family to show up, a young lady appeared with the news that she was Mrs. Peters' helper in the home. "But I'm sure they were not expecting you today," she remarked.

I was beginning to wonder where I might stay for the night, when the Peters arrived. What a surprise to them when they found me on the porch. After chatting a while, we discovered that the telegram the Mission sent informing the Peters of my arrival would come two days after I did. Some introduction to Trinidad! Was this part of learning to trust my heavenly Father when things didn't go as planned?

After a week with this gracious family, I went to the house in Arima where I was to live with another single missionary, Helen Latham, who served as a school teacher for the missionary children as well as doing other tasks. Here's the assignment I was given for my first months: "In the mornings you work in the office on Bible Correspondence courses. At 1:30 p.m. you go out and start visiting house to house. At 5:00 you are free to come home." These rather abrupt instructions from my new field leader would give me a good chance to become acquainted with the people and a new culture. Well, I had been wondering about launching out in a walk of faith. This most definitely was the answer.

Visiting from home to home was interesting to say the least. I couldn't understand the Trinidadian English. In the 50s these people hadn't heard an American accent very often, so they had trouble understanding me, and I was not getting all they were saying. Trinidadians are a very gracious, outgoing people. They would invite me to come and sit on their porch or gallery, or they'd invite me into their homes. Although English is the language the majority in Trinidad speak, I couldn't understand them nor could they understand me at first. Over the weeks, and bit by bit, these ears began to get accustomed to the accent. So you can be sure I was excited one day, after asking the Lord to lead me to people who want to hear about Him, when a very cordial invitation came from the lips of a sweet seven-year old girl.

Eager learners in my outdoor Bible study.

# 7
# First Fruits

I had been praying this prayer quite often, "Lord, You lead me," when a seven-year old girl came up the stairs, and shyly said to me, "Good afternoon, Miss." (You could always count on a formal greeting like that in Trinidad in those early years.) Of course my friend and I answered with our "Good afternoon." Then the girl looked at me with a serious face. "Mommy says, when you finish visiting here, will you come to our house?" I assured her I'd be glad to come.

Soon I was on my way to answer the lady's invitation. She immediately began saying, "You know, I am very strong in my religion but I would like to know what the Bible teaches." Then she asked if I'd be willing to let her invite friends to a Bible study. This was my first experience of teaching Trinidadians in a group. I began asking the Lord what I should teach. The Gospel of John seemed a good place to start because it was new to them. It seemed the Lord did not want me to confront them with accepting Him before they had a better grasp of the Scriptures.

One day the lady I first contacted asked if she could come to my house and talk with me. When she came she said to me, "You know, I really want to ask Jesus into my heart." So I talked further with her, pointing out some of the things this could involve in light of her religious convictions. "I'm not sure," she confided, "that I'm really ready." As I would be coming to her house for class the next week I suggested we'd have time to chat then.

When we next met in her home, I was taken aback with her first response. "I can't accept Jesus." My heart nearly stopped. All along I felt this lady would soon give her life to the Lord. She had witnessed her daughter's conversion and was aware of her Christian leadership in Trinidad. I wondered at the sudden change, so when I asked why my new friend could not accept the Lord, she told me, "Because I talked to the family about it—my children, my husband, my brother, my sister— and they all said that if you leave your religion and follow Jesus, we will never speak to you again. The cost is too great." I looked my new friend in the eye and said, "I agree with you that it is going to cost you, but if you don't ask the Lord Jesus into your heart, your fate would be awful since the Scriptures teach that the horrors of an eternal hell await all who refuse Him." "Will you give me another week?" she asked, "I need to consider this again." So I went away feeling at least a little encouraged. But I couldn't stop crying. I kept on praying. Then, about the middle of the week, a single lady around 20 years old who was attending the class, appeared at my door. She named the religious woman and said, "That lady sent me to tell you that she had asked the Lord Jesus into her heart."

This dear person had kept on studying the Bible. In our visits she revealed God had been working in her heart. She shared, "You know, every night for years as I knelt by my bed, I would always pray one prayer, 'Lord Jesus, if I'm not in the right way, then will you show me the right way?'" Then she added, "You know, it isn't what you said, but what God's Word has said." That was a tremendous encouragement. God was beginning to show me, even though I was visiting many different people, not all would respond positively. He was the One doing the work. All I had to do was be willing to be a *"corn of wheat"* that would fall into the soil and die and soon I would rise to vibrant new life. Thank You Lord! Years later I came across this woman again. Her faith was strong even though her husband had not made the commitment to Jesus.

In one of the children's Bible classes held on the front porch of a religious but non-Christian home, I met a young girl, Mala, who was a very young Christian. I had taken over this study from a missionary friend, Mary Heppner, who became ill and was returning to Canada. There was already some good fruit from the children's classes. Here I had come to Trinidad supposedly to teach and encourage such as this babe in Christ. Instead, she was the channel God used to teach me many lessons.

Mala did not hide the fact that she had trusted Jesus for salvation. Because of this, the neighbors had mocked her father. "Why, you can't even control your young daughter. She's now following the Christian way." Severe persecution of Mala took on several forms. First, she was not allowed to attend our Bible classes. Her parents believed that this Edith Johnson had put an evil spirit on her. They were sure that if their daughter were kept away from the missionary she would return to the family's religion. Keeping Mala from me didn't work. They beat her and threw her Bible into the fire.

As the persecution intensified, God spoke to my heart. "If you want to love and minister to these people, you will have to suffer." After seeing the relatives heap verbal abuse on Mala, I decided to talk to her father. When I confronted him, God gave me the needed boldness. I went away with the assurance that Mala would now have liberty to choose her religion. However, the persecution only grew worse. Returning from a short holiday, I had a premonition that a hard situation would only become harder. It was then that I learned that the very morning that I left, Mala's father flew into a rage, took a heavy leather strap and began to beat Mala. "I will continue to do this until you promise to quit following the Christian way," he threatened. Hearing and seeing the confrontation, the neighbors came running. "Mala, hear what your father is saying and promise your father you'll quit this new religion," they called to her. She bravely responded in tears, "My father can kill me if he wants to, but I still will follow the Christian way." When the beatings seemed of no avail, the family decided to send her to her grandparents in the country. Undoubtedly she would return to the religion of her forefathers, so they figured.

43

After Mala had gone to the country, I felt God would have me take the Mission van and look for her. By nature I have never been a brave, person. Inward struggles of fear often overtake me. What would the father do if he found out? Mala had warned me not to walk in the shadow of any building at night. Her words rang through my mind, "My father will not touch you but he might have someone else attack you." But I knew in my heart that I should visit this precious young girl.

To my utter amazement, the grandmother greeted me warmly and my request to see Mala was granted. I quietly sat and listened to her account. "Mala," I questioned, "What are you going to do?" Without a moment's hesitation, she replied, "Miss Johnson, my father can kill me if he wishes, but I am going to follow the Lord Jesus." Is this what commitment means? Is this part of what learning to walk by faith is? As I was saying goodbye to my little friend, I was utterly taken aback when she told me, "I will see you in Sunday School tomorrow." She explained that there was a big family function with feasting and drinking and she would slip away. "Won't they beat you if they catch you?" I asked. Her response was adamant. "It doesn't matter, I will come."

Cars were few in those days, so when I heard one stop in front of the old wooden lodge where we held services, I was gripped with fear. When the service was over, I walked to the door. There were Mala's uncle and father. I quickly walked to her side and told her what was happening. She wanted to run out the back door but I assured her that the Lord would help us. We would face them together. Then, a very angry uncle walked toward me demanding to talk to the person in charge. I felt that I was the one to whom he should speak. After he poured out some abusive words, I told him, "I see Mala's father is with you and I feel that he's the one to whom I should speak." It was then that I confronted Mala's father, reminding him that he had promised that his child was free to make her choice about religion. No longer did he feel that way. He informed me he would take her home and call the elders of the family together to hear the case. If she returned to the family religion, there would be no further problems. But if she persisted in following the

Christian way, then she would be put out of their home forever. Looking at Mala, I asked if she understood what her father was saying. When she told me she did, she got into the car and left with them.

If you are going to love these people you will have to suffer. If you are going to follow the Saviour, there is no easy way. I could only commit Mala to her Lord.

I had the joy of meeting Mala years later. Although she was still suffering the results of the beatings in earlier years, she was rejoicing in the Lord and still following her heavenly Father.

Pastor Michael Grant with wife Anne.

# 8
# Michael, Young Disciple

The old estate house in Arima, where Helen Latham and I had lived, was far too big for me now that Helen had gone home on furlough. Furthermore, the idea of living alone didn't appeal to me. On the contrary, it depressed me. After a few days of hunting we found a house on 10-foot pillars. I would make my living-quarters upstairs and our few believers would turn the open space underneath into the Arima Evangelical Church. You can't imagine how overjoyed I was that no longer on Sunday mornings would we have to go early to clean the hall, usually left messy from dances and wild parties the night before. I still felt apprehensive about living alone, maybe because I had been in Trinidad for only one year. My fears were needless, however, for my neighbors not only looked out for me but did everything they could to help me.

The good-sized, but unsightly, yard needed much work. But who could I get to help? My friend Matilda, who attended my first Bible class, was quick to respond. "I have just the boy to do the job for you. He can be trusted; he's very reliable." The next day a shy teen by the name of Michael Grant walked into my life.

Life in Trinidad and Tobago was very simple for most living back in the 50s. Michael's father, Felix Grant, worked at an unusual place called Pitch Lake, while he lived in the nearby village of La Brea. The pitch lake is actually a lake where asphalt is dug and refined. The lake is considered by some as a "natural wonder" of the world, though few on the outside world are aware of this phenomenon. Only two other pitch lakes are in existence. Felix's job brought in low wages and required more muscle than skill. Children of the workers, including Michael, would bring lunch at noon for their fathers who worked there.

On one particular day when Michael and his friends were playing a game of cricket close to the lake, Michael's parents drove up and beckoned for him to come to the car. Little did Michael guess what his father was about to tell him. "Son, we are moving from La Brea to a place called Arima. I am getting a better job and will be able to provide more things for you and the family." At his father's urging, Michael got into the car and the family drove away. Wistfully, Michael looked back and waved to his friends. Would he ever see them again? A couple of weeks after their move, my friend Matilda who knew the Felix family, remembered my request for help with the yard.

Michael, wearing tattered clothes and carrying a cutlass in his hand arrived and offered to help clean my yard. As the day progressed, I invited Michael into my simple home for some lunch. He hesitated but then came inside. (He told me later that he had wondered why a white woman was being so kind to him). As I watched him through my window that afternoon, I saw a young man who showed much aptitude and diligence in his work. I knew I wanted him to continue helping me with my yard so I had him come back several times to do other tasks. One day I asked him, "Michael, why don't you come to Sunday School and church?" Michael bowed his head and replied quietly, "Miss I do not have clothes and shoes."

I probed further. "Michael, would you really come if we provided you with these things?"

"Yes, Miss," Michael answered eagerly. With the help of a believer in the congregation, a tailor by trade, Michael soon had some presentable clothes. From that day Michael faithfully attended Sunday School, church and youth meetings at the Hope Evangelical Church.

Excitement was high one Sunday afternoon in January of 1958. An old bus from Arima was making its way to the Queen's

Park Savannah, a large park in Port of Spain, Trinidad's capital city. Among its passengers from the Hope Evangelical Church was Michael Grant. Members of the church were attending the closing service of the Billy Graham Crusade held on the island. That afternoon, Michael joined hundreds who went forward, and invited the Lord Jesus into their lives. Because of his shyness, Michael didn't make this known right then.

Several months later, however, I approached Michael with the question, "Michael, don't you think its about time that you ask Jesus to be your Saviour? You have been attending Hope Church for quite some time."

"Miss, I already have."

"Really Michael, tell me about it."

"When we went to the Billy Graham Crusade."

What welcome words these were to me. Right there I told him that it would be good for us to study the Bible together so that he would grow in his Christian walk. One of the studies we did was Navigator's *Your Decision, Lessons in Assurance*. Michael said this material profoundly impacted his life and still does in his present role as a pastor.

Michael went on to be a diligent and faithful student of the Scriptures. Week after week we continued to meet. Michael always completed his written assignments and his Bible memorization was nothing less than remarkable. It was during that time that Michael got his first real job at the Arima Textile Mill. Being the kind of person that he was, this student carried his faithfulness and diligence into his secular job. God continued to chip and polish Michael's life. I wish you could meet this faithful servant.

When I had to move to another area, Michael received good help from other mentors in our Mission. I remember visiting six months later when Michael made this statement to me, "Miss Johnson, I can talk now."

"What do you mean by that?" I asked him.

"Well, the Lord has helped me and I can stand up and give my testimony and I can even lead a service. You know, Miss, I have been thinking about how you left your home and came to Trinidad to teach us about the Lord Jesus, and that we should be willing to do the same. I am going to go to Bible School and become a pastor."

"But how are you going to get the money?"

"I know God will supply what I need," he answered cheerfully.

There was no doubt about the fact that in his early years Michael needed some coaching on financial matters. Often the Grant's larder got pretty sparse. The reason? Michael gave most of his meager income to the work of the Lord and kept little for himself.

Maybe this preacher-to-be understood the spirit of what Paul told the Corinthian believers, *"God loveth a cheerful giver."*

This one-time yard boy has since grown tall physically and tall in the ways of His Master. He trained at the Jamaica Bible College, married a fine Christian girl, Ann Nanton, who was saved in the San Juan Church, and they went on to pastor several local churches. He also has served as Moderator of the churches in the islands of Trinidad and Tobago, and went on to be National Superintendent of the English islands where World Team has been working since 1949. Michael has had many opportunities to teach in Christian Education courses. He spent two years at a Christian university in Columbia, SC where he received his Master's degree. He has been involved in church-related projects such as Ridgewalk Camp and Conference Center (Chapter 17). He's seen churches split as well as grow. He has given endless counsel to church committees and pastors on a variety of subjects. Together this couple have gone through illnesses, times of struggle and trials, and have come through them all.

Michael's life testifies to the strong grip of the Lord on him. Nearing retirement now, Michael and Ann continue their life-long burden of bringing West Indians into the kingdom and giving wise counsel and encouragement to pastors and lay people alike. Michael is a beautiful example of one insignificant *"corn of wheat"* falling into the ground and dying so that others might live.

# 9

# A Dream Comes True

"It seems best, Miss Johnson, that you go back to the States early to regain your health." I could hardly believe what I was hearing. I was short four months of a supposed four-year term. The years of living in the tropics and no doubt my active lifestyle (I had gained the name, "Speedy Edie"), had taken its toll. So the year 1959 found me back home trying to regain my health.

"Father, it would be such a great help for me to have my own car in Trinidad." I guess my silent plea came from sheer fatigue as I thought back on those beginning years in the tropics. Not only had I gone on foot for all my visits the first two years, I had a bike for the remaining 18 months and I had done it all in 85 to 100 degree heat. I didn't realize my body wasn't up to that kind of punishment. "Just think how many more people I could tell about You, Father," I convincingly prayed, "and I wouldn't have to walk or ride my bike everywhere."

I decided that I would ask the Lord to provide a car, but never once make the need known to anyone. And I wanted God to bring this about without ever doubting that it was His doing. Often in the year I had reminded the Lord of this need. I hadn't seen a hint of it happening, however, and I had already started back to Trinidad. As I was returning to the areas where Muriel Hayne and I had done home mission work, Prince George and Rolla BC, I couldn't help savouring those early experiences of never-to-be-forgotten friendships that became part of my life. I was full of excitement at seeing old friends again.

So, starting in Prince George, BC I planned to visit my dear friends Ann and John Esau. Would they even be living there now?

About the first thing Ann did when I pulled into her home was hand me a letter. She wanted to prove that they were indeed thinking of me, but had held the letter because of no address. "You have not heard from us for five years," Ann's surprise letter said. She confided that she had something important to talk about, so she invited me to come back in the evening when John would be home. Naturally I looked forward to visiting them again.

So when I returned to their little wood-frame house, I clearly recalled the children's Bible class I held there some five years back. After we greeted one another, she looked me in the eye and said, "Edith, do you need a car?"

Startled, I responded, "Ann, why do you ask?"

Her next words were, "God has laid it separately on John's heart as well as mine, that if you need a car we are going to buy one for you. But let's wait until John comes home from work as I know he wants us to share together the plan we have." Can you imagine what went on in my heart the next hours? Had I not asked God to supply the car without having to make the need known? And God was going to do it in such a way that I would never doubt that He alone did it. Thankfulness overwhelmed me. Here again was the assurance that the God I love and serve had heard my petition. This faith thing was a step by step experience.

Sitting at the dinner table now, John was adding to what Ann had told me. "When you return to Trinidad, we do not want you to even think of looking at used cars." John was a good mechanic and it was without question that I find a brand new car of my choosing. "We will send you a check to cover the cost." Was I dreaming or was this real? Not only did the Esaus live in a small wood frame house, they had a small service station with a little shed at the back. John repaired cars while Ann serviced the gas pumps at the front, even when it was 35 degrees below zero. Can you imagine the thrill it would be for me to return to Trinidad with the cash on hand to buy a brand new car, and then to drive one?

Almost 15 years later, I was again in the Esau's home for Sunday lunch. Only now the home had been remodelled and was simply beautiful. John asked this question, "Edith, would you like to know the other side of the story about that first car we bought for you?"

I assured him I would and carefully listened while John told me an amazing story.

"As you know, God had laid it on Ann's and my heart that if you needed a car we were to buy it. At the time, our house was badly in need of repair. As we prayed about it, I decided I would place the responsibility of the decision on Ann as she is a lady who dearly loves her home. As we chatted together, her response was, 'John, if God wants us to buy that car there is no decision to be made. We will buy the car.'

"We mortgaged the gas station and as time went on, we re-paid the loan. The day finally came when I told Ann, 'We can take out another mortgage and repair the house.' When the man came to do the work, he went up into the attic and came down shaking his head. 'John, I am simply amazed that the roof of this house did not collapse this past winter under the pressure of all that snow. It seems everything is rotted out up there.' My response was simply, 'I know Who held it up.'"

My heart was deeply moved as I learned how God was teaching me His awesome ways, building up my faith. When I looked at the couple He had used and the sacrifices they had made, I struggled to hold back the tears.

Our first of six church plants, a humble beginning.

# 10
# Teamwork

When I arrived back in Trinidad, one of the first things I did was to buy my "dream" car—yes, the first brand new car I ever owned, a small Ford. But added to this answer, something very special happened at the beginning of that term. It was the fall of 1962 and the Lord was going to give me a co-worker. I couldn't wait to meet this Donna Williamson from Coeur d'Alene, Idaho. It wasn't without some apprehension though. Would I like her? Would she like me? Could we work together? Could we live together in harmony? Would she be bossy?

Donna shares a bit about her arrival. "When I arrived at the airport in Trinidad it was dark and had been raining. As I was about to get in to what I thought was the passenger side of the car, I was startled to find the steering wheel facing me. So I quickly backed up and stepped right into a gutter. Edith quickly grabbed my arm. I could imagine the Trinidad newspaper coming out the next morning with the headline, 'Missionary Pulls Co-worker from Gutter.'"

But the Lord had prepared us for an unusual ministry together in Trinidad. It was amazing how God blended our lives. I had never seen Donna before. She had a Scandinavian background. I had a Scandinavian background. I loved to go fishing; she loved fishing. I graduated from Prairie Bible Institute; Donna graduated from Prairie. God put us on a team. In fact, this was before West Indies Mission (World Team) ever became team-minded. They published a leaflet later with pictures of both of us stating that we were the first team that had been put together in our Mission. They saw how our gifts complemented one another as we planted churches in Trinidad.

So while Donna was still struggling with jet lag, we were to hold a youth retreat in the village of Toco on Trinidad's north coast. God had given me the privilege of seeing EYF (Evangelical Youth Fellowship) come into being and I was to direct our first Carnival Retreat. Donna came to the retreat with me but I was disturbed when the girls came to me with the report, "All Miss Williamson wants to do is sleep, and she sleeps so soundly that even our noise doesn't wake her." Was this the help that God had given me?

With my active nature, could we relate peacefully and be a team that could lead? Once Donna had recovered from jet lag, and with her first exposure to the tropics, she proved that my fears were groundless.

Seventeen years later when Donna left the island, I stood with tears running down my face. But in the between time, God had much in store for both of us. I soon began to recognize that God had much to teach me through the one He had led into my life. In many ways she became a balance for me, and to this day both she and her husband Max are dearly loved "family" members.

San Juan was a heavily populated area just outside the capital, Port of Spain. Our beginnings in San Juan were no different from beginnings in other places; we first had to find a house to rent. At our first place we had a terrible time getting rid of the grease that was ground into the floor. After we rolled up our sleeves and did some much needed scrubbing and painting, it had the earmarks of a livable home, that is until we arrived back from our Carnival retreat. It didn't take many minutes to discover our home had been broken into. I found everything ransacked and generally topsy-turvy.

All the places that we had rented had required extensive clean up. So I asked the Lord one day, "Father, why don't you give us clean houses to rent?" As these cleaning bees continued, my question was answered. People were watching these women from abroad doing the things other foreigners wouldn't think of doing—scrubbing floors, washing windows, painting walls—whatever it took to make a house a home. "Why are these women so different? What are they going to do when the work in the house is completed? Where are their husbands?" Our prayer had been, "Lord, give us contact with these people." When visitation began we were labelled as very different from the average. God would use this difference to give us some great openings.

In a year we moved to a second home in San Juan. "When you are settled in your new home in San Juan will you come and teach religious instruction at our secondary school?" a student friend asked me one day. In San Juan, heavily populated as it was, we were learning to navigate quite well and soon had come to know quite a number of people. The young student went on to tell me that the principal had said, "Tell the ladies that if they come we will give them complete liberty to teach the Bible to the students." With much excitement I ran to share the wonderful news with Donna.

As we thought about the possibility of teaching Bible in the secondary school, we wanted to hunt up some English-speaking believers from the island of St. Vincent who were in the hills that surround San Juan. How good it would be to have them as a part of our San Juan church.

Soon we were meeting in our living room for Sunday morning services, as well as for prayer meetings. It was time now to walk through the door that God was opening at the secondary school. With increased numbers and an outgrown living room, we prayed that after we got to know the school principal, we would be able to ask him if we could rent the premises on Sunday mornings. Didn't this seem like the diplomatic thing to do?

"Mr. Mootoo, we are the ladies our student friend spoke to you about who can offer religious instruction once a week in your school." Had we been too bold? Our fears vanished when he replied, "I am delighted to have you. Please sit down so we can chat."

After stating his pleasure again at our willingness to teach the students the Scriptures, we thanked him and were about to leave. "Please stay a few more minutes." I wondered what else he wanted. We wondered if he was going to allow us to see the outworking of the promise, "Before they call, I will answer and while they are yet speaking I will hear,"?

"Ladies, would you like to use this building for weekends?"

"How much would the rent be?" I asked.

"Oh, there will be no charge. The building stands vacant on the weekends." God had blown our diplomacy to bits and provided the home for the budding San Juan Evangelical Church for the next three years. Since the school did not have electricity, the church agreed we should wire the building so we could have Sunday evening services as well as prayer meetings. We were beginning to grow and Donna and I were one happy team.

# 11
# Fresh Footprints

San Juan had a reputation for gangs of rough young fellows. As believers we made a decision to ask God to give us contact with these needy men. As the Sunday evening service was coming to a close, there was a clomp, clomp, clomp that decidedly interrupted the meeting. Six men stomped into the room with hats pulled down over their heads. After making a good bit of noise, they seated themselves. It was quite obvious that God was answering our prayers—in His unique way. We were startled and disappointed that two men in the congregation demanded we call the police. "We can't do that, God is answering our prayers," Donna and I told the two brothers.

For several Sunday nights these rowdies kept appearing and each week they arrived a little earlier. One night they actually were on time; we were so happy!

Later we learned they had come intending to break up the service. Before too many weeks passed, four of the six turned their lives over to Jesus. One of the new converts became a lay preacher and another started a Bible training center next door to his home.

Vacation time for Donna and me gave us a needed break. A conviction grew in my heart which I finally verbalized to Donna. "When we come back from vacation, Mr. Mootto (the school principal) is going to tell us he has decided to emigrate to Canada. Where would our growing congregation relocate? Was God asking us to make a fresh footprint in the path of faith?" True to the information God had impressed on my heart, the day we returned, Mr. Mootto appeared at our door. "I want you ladies to have first chance to buy the school building. I have to sell it as I plan to move to Canada."

Questions arose immediately. Where would we go? How would God supply?

We were hard pressed to get any money as offerings were so meager? "There are churches in Canada and the U.S. that give loans at low rates to missions, even with no interest," suggested a fellow missionary. "Great," I answered "but you will have to show me where those churches are."

Interestingly, every time I began to pray about a loan, a pastor's name came to mind. But he doesn't have money and besides, his church is small. I pushed the thought aside. More likely than not, my eyes were more fixed on the pastor than on the Lord.

A little later, with considerable fear, I wrote the pastor in question explaining our situation. "Would you know of a church that would consider giving a loan?" When the pastor wrote back he told me quite assuredly, "I will go to the bank and take out a loan in my name for your church. Two men have agreed they will repay half of the loan if your congregation can pay the other half." I shouldn't have been surprised since we had made this a matter of prayer. Our small church group was bonding together as brothers and sisters in Christ. Offerings often fell short of our commitment, but God never let us down. Giving nearly doubled. We were all blessed in this joint venture and the church overseas that had promised to underwrite much of the cost, rejoiced that they had a part.

Trinidadian law says that you can't evict a tenant unless you find a suitable place that he will agree to rent. The church had instructed Donna and me to contact a realtor. "Ladies," he told us, "I do not have anything. Most lots have buildings on them." We were leaving with heavy hearts when he called back, "I do have one old house for sale but I didn't want to say too much as the tenant refuses to move out." Both mission leaders and our church group advised us against buying the house. Not a good proposition.

One Sunday shortly after, we were singing a hymn and the Lord seemed to be saying to me, "I want you to buy that property even with the man in the house. This morning, rather than give the message you had planned, encourage My people to step out in faith. I caused the Jordan to roll back when the priest stepped in. I will do the same for you."

I began to reason with the Lord, "What if...what if?" Turning to the congregation I opened the Book of Joshua and told them *"Step into the waters of Jordan"* and see God work. After the service I shared what I believed God was saying concerning the house.

The church suggested we go back the next morning and offer $10,000 (T & T currency) for the building but not one cent more. He told us that becoming the owner of the building would give us the first option to buy the land. The realtor's assistant said, "If I ask the man to come here would you be willing to make him that offer?"

"Yes," we replied.

The realtor's response was clear, "I can't even think of that amount." Then he dropped his head and we all sat in silence. It seemed we had come to the end of our road, but God's road hadn't closed. The man looked up at us and said, "Alright, I'll sell it to you at that price."

"Those foolish white ladies think they can get that man to move," laughed the neighbors. "They will learn." That building had been bought and sold four times. After the church had instructed us to make our offer for the house, they suggested, "We will pray and you two go talk to the man." We went to see the renter and laid out our plan. Four weeks later the keys to an empty house were ours.

Excitement was high and the growing church in San Juan began two tasks, converting the lower part of the building into a place for the church to worship and preparing the upper portion for Donna and me. Wheel barrows were put to work and buckets of dirt were hauled away, so we thought. After a heavy nights' rain, most of the soil had washed back under the building. We hadn't allowed space for drainage.

As we were getting the final touches on the church, I was using an electric sander and realized too late that I had stepped on damp concrete. I screamed "Somebody help me! Somebody help me!" as electricity surged through my body. I tried to throw off the sander but in a couple of seconds I was thrown backwards breaking the electric connection. God spared my life. What a close call. I was so thankful for God's intervention and that I had suffered no lasting effects.

Just imagine the opening of our very humble but adequate church building! It was a day of rejoicing in San Juan and another milestone in the planting of the church in Trinidad.

# 12
# Miracles in Marabella

We both had been in our homelands for a year so when we flew back to our adopted home, we faced a brand new challenge. The ECWI (Evangelical Church of the West Indies) had one isolated church in southern Trinidad in a town called Siparia. The Mission's instructions were somewhat unusual, "We want you to locate in another area of the south and plant a church there."

We decided on Marabella, just outside of San Fernando, the second largest city in Trinidad. Several reasons pointed to this ideal location. The size of the house we located was just right but the broken windows and doors stared us in the face. We prayed, "Father, here's a vandalized house, but why do you want us to rent this one?" (Young fellows had used this place to do their drugs). After a month of hard work, this rented house on Centeno Street became our home. Scores of people passing wondered why these ladies did not hire maids to do all the dirty work. Neighbors came by with words of warning. "Every car on this street has had its battery stolen and some of the houses have been broken into. You better be careful!" In the days ahead, we experienced both.

Knowing some of these problems from experience, a good friend, Mr. Ramkisoon, offered us one of his dogs. He cleaned up Jimbo, and presented him to us. It seems that this dog was in the habit of swimming across the river to the oil refinery in search of scraps that the workers left from their lunches. In the process, Jimbo got his coat full of oil so that we dared not touch him. This left a certain amount of oil and debris on our front porch, his favorite resting place. All of this, however, paid off the night Jimbo heard the side window of our car being smashed. He gave chase and we were happy to discover that our car battery was still in its bracket.

A few weeks later, when we walked into our kitchen to start breakfast, we found the back door standing wide open. To my horror, there was a sturdy plank leaning against the back of the house leading up to the guest room window. It so happened that a woman from Portland, Oregon had arrived for a visit the day before. As we raced up the stairs, all was quiet in her room and we thought she might be missing. We carefully opened the door, only to hear, "I thought you said I could sleep in." We announced that we had had an intruder in the night, much to her disbelief, until she found her watch was missing from the night stand. The miracle of the night was that she slept through it. The door on the stand always had an annoying squeak and no matter how we tried, we could never open it quietly. She had also put her purse in the closet with all of her travel documents and money. They were not taken! We wonder what could have happened had she awakened. So, whether it was the sound sleep (the tropics can do this to a visitor from abroad) or the chloroform that some intruders use on people, we know it was God's guardian angels who protected the three women in the house that night. Though we were uneasy about the new location, we knew we had to trust God for His protection in this situation. Jimbo, our faithful watch dog, was a needed provision too.

A wide open door best describes this new opportunity in Marabella. The first day we visited Ma and Pa Ramkissoon, they told us, "We belong to another religion but our children are nothing. Please take them and teach them the Christian way." They had eight children, and with others coming to our living room, we soon outgrew our space. Sunday School, morning worship and a prayer service, challenged us to *"Ask, and it will be given to you"* (Matt 7:7). There had to be a novel way to enlarge our quarters.

"Ladies, there is an auto company here, Neil and Massey, that imports disassembled cars. For $25 you can buy a whole truckload of the crates the cars come in." We were also told that one truckload would be enough to enclose the downstairs. This would give us what we needed for a chapel. Can you imagine our delight the day a truck pulled up in front of our house loaded with crates? *"Faithful is He who calls you, who also will do it."*

But wait a minute! None of the hundreds of nails had been pulled from the boards. What in the world were we going to do? Without questioning, we knew the bright idea came from the Father of Light. We would buy a sheet of plywood and set up a table for ping pong games and invite the young people to each pull out nails for one hour at a time. It worked. Soon we had a heap of plywood without nails and we noticed the youth group multiplying quite rapidly. The young people also chipped and rolled the asphalt to make a decent floor for the downstairs chapel.

About the time we were thinking of enclosing the chapel, the man across the street directed us to an older carpenter by the name of Harry whom he felt would be a good help in our project. Often when we chatted with Harry the conversation would turn to the difference between having religion or having a relationship with the person of Jesus. From the day we first met Harry he was showing a great deal of interest in our project, in fact quite a bit more than we expected. Every so often he asked us where we would find land to build a church. Some times after work he would come and help us look for land. As proof, the Marabella church today sits on land that Mr. Harry located for us.

Not long after this, the Marabella young people asked if they could put on a drama and invite people in from the neighborhood. We asked them what their drama would depict. We were aware that most of the players who attended the chapel were not yet believers, so we told them. "Write out your drama so we can see it." They tried without success. "We can't do that. We don't know how. Let us tell you what it is about and we think you will feel good about it." So these eager teens portrayed a part of Trinidadian life all too familiar to them—an alcoholic father who was abusive to his wife, and a pastor admonishing the wayward father. The play was an immediate winner. The boys amazed us with their acting. Soon the two who had taken the parts of the pastor and the abusive father were so convicted by the truth they were portraying that they both prayed for forgiveness and salvation. Some of the people who came to the presentation continued coming to the chapel. Later we had the joy of hearing them confess their faith in Christ.

Another plus during this time was that one of the Ramkissoons' children asked Jesus into his life, then another, until eventually all were walking with the Lord. One has since become a pastor in Trinidad and another is assistant to a pastor in Canada. From this youth group in Marabella four are pastors today.

The boarded-in chapel became too small in a matter of weeks. So once again Donna and I took the need to our heavenly Father. One day we noticed that two men were hauling a knocked-down building on their truck and we asked each other, "Where did they get that building? Just maybe we could go that route." We found out that Texaco was selling off their old bungalows. Next time there is an auction, we decided to go. So we talked to a Christian man, Joe Bennett who worked at Texaco and asked him to notify us next time there was a sale.

We were also pleased to discover about this time that our friend Harry had started attending services at the Marabella Church.

In a few days Joe Bennett called to tell us that the next day there would be another auction. Donna gathered all the money she had and I gathered all I had, certainly not enough to impress an auctioneer. We contacted our missionary colleague, Ben Penner, who was pretty knowledgeable about the structure of buildings. With Ben's addition to the money pot, we now had a little less than $1,000 (T & T currency or around $250 US). With the prices the bungalows were going at, I said to Donna, "Lets' go home." After a pause she suggested, "We've been here all afternoon, we'd better stay a little longer." In my heart I said, "Thank you, Father," even though I wasn't happy.

So the auctioneer began calling for bids again and we thought we shouldn't go too high so we said to Ben, offer this much. Immediately the auctioneer called out "Going, going, gone". Ben had the last bid and we had the bungalow. What a miracle! The auctioneer assured us that we had one awesome bargain.

The best part about this was that through our very helpful new friend, Harry, who had first suggested we go this route, we now had the building that would help complete the church in Marabella. After several weeks of Harry's work, our little chapel was finished and we were in the middle of an evangelistic crusade. We had been praying fervently that Mr. Harry would come to know Jesus. Saturday night we gave out the tract, "Which Church Saves?" Harry again told us as he had many times, "I will go home and peruse this." Sunday morning I had to minister in another church but when I reached home, Donna informed me that Mr. Harry was in church but was very agitated because I was not there. She assured him that she would send me to him as soon as I came home.

That day Mr. Harry became brother Harry. He had thought over his need for a relationship with Jesus Christ and saw that his religion had no power to save. Harry's life now gave evidence to the scriptural truth, *"By their fruits you shall know them."* A very practical man, Harry in every way possible continued to look out for those two women preachers on Centeno Street.

Marabella had turned a corner and there was no doubt about it, the Lord Jesus was building His church.

One-time fisherman guide, Tallboy, and his daughters.

Ben Penner and I with our big catch

# 13
# A Real Fish Story

Donna and I loved to fish. My dad had taken me fishing when I was little. Donna's father taught her how to fish, and they often went fishing together in Idaho. We had tried snorkeling our first term and marvelled at what we saw in the tropical ocean. We were quite ready this term to try fishing. We asked our friend Pa Ramkisoon if he knew someone who could take us fishing. "I know just the one," Pa quickly offered. Shortly after, Pa had a tall man in tow. "I want you to meet Tallboy (the nickname wasn't by chance)," Pa said. "With confidence I can put you ladies in this man's hands—best fisherman I know."

Some months before this encounter, something unusual happened. One day under his little shelter where he sold his fish, Tallboy quickly straightened his tall frame and hit his head so hard that he almost passed out. He prayed, "Oh God, do something for me. I need help." The very day this happened, he arrived at our house. As we talked together I felt that God would have me give him a Bible. I found one and gave it to him, not knowing that this day was his 33rd birthday. He accepted it as a birthday gift, later telling me that no one in his entire life had ever given him a gift for his birthday. Always helpful at church to the two of us, he told us that he would someday get saved, but didn't want to do so until God had really convicted him.

It seemed that day had come, and his face showed he truly meant it. He confessed to me, "I'm ready. God has convicted me." It was not long after that we saw the fruits of grace in this new brother's life.

The morning arrived that Tallboy was all geared up to take us fishing. He not only took us fishing, he spoiled us. He put the bait on the hooks, he took out the hooks and scaled the fish as well.

One day I had to exercise faith a little more than usual because of a promise I made. Our churches had a group of kids camping in the country and I said to the cook, "Mamma Davis, Donna and I are going to catch fish Monday evening. We are going to clean them and we'll bring them to you early Tuesday morning so that you can prepare them for the children's lunch."

With the counsellors at camp we were forty-five in all. So I went to our new fisherman and asked him, "Will you please take us fishing We need to catch enough to feed forty children at the campout." Tallboy told us, "Ladies, I have bad news for you. I have caught very few fish today. I have fished these waters for years and I have found that when the water is this murky color you never catch fish."

I said, "Brother Tallboy, but where would we get fish for over 40 people? We do not have the money to buy fish and we told Mamma D we would supply the fish."

We jumped into the boat and Brother Tallboy took us to all the good spots he knew, yet the fish weren't biting. Finally he said, "It's going to be dark soon and I know of only one more spot. We will try that and if we don't get a bite, we will head for shore." So when we dropped our two lines overboard (each line had two hooks) at this spot, we pulled in two at a time until we had enough fish for two meals. What a fabulous catch!

With hearts full of thanks to our Father and to our fisherman friend, we headed home. We promised Mamma D that the fish would be cleaned. With the help of Brother Tallboy and a neighbor, all the fish were cleaned. Some of my excitement left me because I was fighting an upset stomach. I told Donna "Never let me do this again, please."

It was a year later and there was another camp. Evidently I forgot how sick I had been, because I was even willing to clean the fish once more. This time we caught fish right away, and were able to provide the kids with fried fish once more. Was this another little step in learning to trust God? And by the way, that was the last time I made any promise about cleaning fish!

Whenever Brother Tallboy was able to take us fishing, we found the outing a source of relaxation. But he was a blessing to many of his other friends as well—especially to those who passed by his fish stand. He was well equipped and even when he didn't plan to go out to fish, he would stay by his stand and give a gospel tract to everybody who passed by.

One day Tallboy came to me with a serious proposition. "Miss Johnson, where I live there is no Sunday School, there is not even a church we can go to. You must come and start a Sunday School in Williamsville." I said, "Brother Tallboy, if God has put that on your heart, then you must take responsibility. Once you start, if the going gets rough, you can't quit." I told him that we would help him but he must take the lead. He slowly agreed, knowing that this would be a brand new step with God. When he did start the Sunday School, God saw his willingness and honored him. He held his first Sunday School in the open space under the house (the house was on pillars). Running out of space for classes, he suggested that the class meet under the nearby bridge. He was quite aware that there could be a problem should it rain, the creek would rise too quickly and too high and the class would have to squeeze under the house for that day.

Once a heavy drinker and for years a gambler, Tallboy now had a purpose for life. He fished to provide food for a living, but he had now become a fisher of men.

Ruby loves her "brimmed hats."

# 14
# Lady with the Broad-brimmed Hat

One of the extras in our life in the West Indies was the day that Ruby Thompson walked into our lives.

I had heard that Ruby and Franklin Thompson were a gracious couple. When one of World Team's missionaries was ill, it was the Thompsons, long associated with a group of excellent churches in Trinidad, who took our fellow missionary into their home and nurtured him back to health. In a short time after that, wedding bells announced the marriage of this same young man. As I sat at the wedding reception, I noticed a tall lady wearing a very broad-brimmed hat. Someone pointed out that this was Ruby Thompson.

We were about to finish planning our second ladies' retreat when the discussion came up, "Who will be the speaker for next year's retreat?" I suggested Ruby Thompson. I told our committee I had found out that she was a high school principal, and an excellent speaker with a remarkable testimony. Besides, she was the mother of four energetic young people. Donna and I were to contact her. It was Franklin, her husband, who enthusiastically recommended that she would be just the one to take on such an assignment. He was right. When she came to the Victory Heights Retreat Center, an overflow group was there to welcome her. It so happened that Ruby was assigned to the same tent that Donna and I were in. Never in my wildest dreams could I have imagined how God would bond our lives together for years to come.

We arranged after the retreat to have Ruby spend a weekend at the beach house that served as a vacation spot for the Trinidad World Team family. It was while chatting that I mentioned my desire to someday go to Barbados (an island north of us) to a Keswick Convention. You ought to have seen Ruby's reaction at the word Keswick. She jumped up out of her seat and looked at me and asked, "Are you interested in Keswick?" I said, "Very much so." Then we got talking about the possibility of having Keswick Conventions in Trinidad. (That became a reality in 1974 and continues to this day). Until his passing, Dr. Stephen Olford spoke at some of Keswick's annual gatherings, and his son David continues his involvement in these and similar conventions in the Caribbean and in North America.

But not only did these deeper life gatherings bring great blessing, Ruby herself became most interested in the work we were carrying on in Trinidad through World Team. So when Ruby asked me not too long after the visit to the beach house, whether I would consider becoming a prayer partner, I was overjoyed. I had already been hoping for that possibility. I just didn't have the courage to ask. Here was a lady in my estimation who was so open and outgoing and was so much a leader, I couldn't imagine her taking time out for me. I had also learned how she had introduced the ministry of Inter-Varsity Christian Fellowship to the schools of our two islands, taking advantage of the open door to religious classes that exists here. Of course they occupied much of Ruby's spare time. So with this in mind I felt very honored to pray on a daily basis with her and assured her that she could count on me. At this point Ruby gave me an unusual invitation, "You have to have someplace where you have a home base. I want you to know that day or night you can come to our house. There will always be a bed for you. You will always have perfect liberty to go into the refrigerator or prepare yourself a meal. Our home will become your home when you are away from yours in the States." All of these years I have enjoyed the Thompson's "open home" policy, understanding that

I could come and go as I please. I often gave thanks to God for this home away from home.

Did our friendship always go smoothly? Oh no. Ruby has a very strong personality. And so do I. There have been times through the years where we would crash head on. Then too, she was from a culture that I was learning, and I was from a culture she didn't know too much about. As a result, we often had misunderstandings. But I thank the Lord that we never let the sun go down on our anger.

Let me explain how our partnership in prayer works. We began by spending time once a week together. It was in those early days that the Lord took Franklin home through strokes and then a major heart attack. This brought us even closer together, and we began to use the telephone. In the mornings I would call her at 6:00 and we would pray. At 9:30 in the evening I would expect a call from Ruby. We would chat a bit about how the day went, pray together and say goodnight. These two encounters a day left a deep imprint on my life. As the years have gone by I have found Ruby to be a woman of stalwart faith, one who has walked with me through hard places. Often, her partnership meant setting aside her own agenda. Many a time we met to share names and burdens and other requests. Sometimes we set aside a day of prayer in a park, or where we swim in the ocean. Other times we fasted. What a privilege to be prayer-partners and see God work in ways we little dreamed.

And I know you have one more question to ask concerning Ruby. Does she still wear that broad-brimmed hat? Absolutely! In Trinidad it fits her lifestyle to a T.

Marabella Church began in our front room

# 15
# Do Angels Use Telephones?

A new trial was waiting for us as we made our move into San Fernando, the second largest city on the island. We were considering a new area called Pleasantville. However, housing in this new area was harder to find. When we lived in areas close to our churches, we usually got many new contacts. But in San Fernando, no one knew us. Let me explain a little further. Because our Trinidadian people are a very friendly, gracious folk, we expected to find the same in Pleasantville. As we began visiting, we expected the usual "Ladies, come in and have a seat." To turn our talk to spiritual things was usually quite easy since Trinidadians are normally God-fearing people.

How strange it seemed in Pleasantville not to be warmly welcomed into their homes. Was our faithfulness as well as our faith being tested? Is this where God wants us to be His instruments to plant a church? After months of wrestling with indifference, our Mission leadership suggested, "Maybe you would do better in Siparia. That church is really struggling and has requested you to work with them."

One more time to face housing needs. "Father, please give us a clean house that we can move into." Driving from San Fernando to Siparia we came across an attractive house that was being built. Wouldn't it be nice, for a change, to move into one that is presentable like this one appears to be. The few believers in Siparia joined us in our house-hunting project. God had a surprise waiting for us. I wonder if He smiled when we found out what He was about to do?

Involved in a second week of prayer to launch the new year, I was mystified by a remark a lady put to me,"So you are going to be my new neighbor?" Thinking she was referring to our move to Siparia, I told her, "Yes, when we find a house." With amazement she queried, "Aren't you going to take the house my neighbor, Mr. Clock, is building?" Donna was soon listening to what I was hearing. "There must be a mistake since we know nothing about a house," we continued. The lady responded, "The owner has received three telephone calls saying he must not rent the house to anyone else because you want it. In fact, he has turned down three others who wanted the house."

A few minutes later we were standing in front of the house calling out our Trinidadian greeting, "Good night, Mr. Clock (nickname given to the gentleman because he had one long arm and one short arm)."

"Good night," he replied, "why didn't you come yesterday as agreed? I have turned away three parties, having received three phone calls telling me about you ladies." Mr. Clock seemed quite annoyed. As I gave expression to the thought that there must be two other white missionaries involved, Mr. Clock strongly objected. "No, you two ladies are the ones for whom I have been keeping the house." Shortly after the encounter, we rented this amazing new house.

Questions flooded our minds. Who had spoken on our behalf? After many attempts to find out who our mediator was, it still remained a mystery. Do angels use telephones, we wondered? I am finding that God will go to any length to teach His children to trust Him.

The General Council of the English-speaking Caribbean fields of World Team, gave us a little proposition in our going into Siparia. "We will give you one year in Siparia and then evaluate your work. If things remain the same, we will have to sell the property and move you to another area." With those words ringing in our ears, we joined hearts and hands with the few believers and together we gave ourselves to prayer and to the work.

An unfinished church building, a property that had the smell of marijuana and had been used for immoral purposes (sound familiar?) confronted us. We will *"arise and build."* God had seen Nehemiah through a lot more than we faced. He would do the same for us.

When our time was up and we were ready to leave Siparia, God confirmed that He had wanted us there. Always the desire was in our hearts that God would work in such a way that we could leave a church with a local pastor. Can you imagine what happened the day we left? God had not only supplied a resident pastor, Hobson Nicholson and his wife, but this was the first church in our association that would be taking on the pastor's full support. How faithful is our God!

As to the mysterious phone call, whether angel or human, I'm trusting we'll be able to thank them when we get to the other side.

Ridgewalk Camp
Cabins were built by local volunteers and help from Canada & USA.

# 16

# Camping
# Growth of a Vision

Camping was in my blood as far back as I can remember. Saturday after Saturday I would go with my father to a camp that was being built in Washington State, Lake Retreat Conference Grounds. After Dad would pack up his little tribe, he would drive us to this beautiful spot and give himself to the job at hand. Since this camping venture was still in the making, we kids had the freedom to run all over the campgrounds. How we looked forward to these breaks from home. How mother must have looked forward to the break as well.

I've already told you about living only a few miles from Lake Sammamish Bible Camp and how that impacted my life as a youth. Each summer I experienced afresh the work of God's Spirit in my life. I will always thank a faithful Sunday School teacher for making that week possible, especially through those depression years when my parents could not afford the modest cost of one week of camp.

Then as I ministered with the Canadian Sunday School Mission those two unforgettable years in northern BC after my years of Bible School, a brand new opportunity presented itself. A special couple with whom I had become acquainted by the name of George and Nellie Campbell, who lived a little north of Prince George, BC, surprised my co-worker and me by writing us a rather unusual letter. "Do you think the CSSM would be interested in building a Bible camp for the children and young people here at Ness Lake? We have a piece of land on the lake we'd like to donate for that purpose."

I wasted no time writing the BC Director of the CSSM, Pastor Henry Unrau. Within a few days he and his wife arrived at Ness Lake. I remember waiting to go to the site, praying that the leaky boat would get us across to the property. The passenger manifest included George and Nellie Campbell, Henry and Jennie Unrau and their small son, Muriel Hayne and myself. What an amazing journey. Quite possibly we would be putting our feet on the land that some day might well become a famous Bible Camp in BC.

The six of us knelt together at the water's edge and asked God to make the dream of the Campbells a reality. Little did I think that the next year I would have the task of fighting the mosquitoes, drinking muddy water dosed with chlorox and counselling a group of lively girls. A grand total of 99 children had arrived to taste camping at its best.

One of the early couples who got involved was John and Gwen Reimer. God used these stalwarts along with many others, in the physical development of Ness Lake Camp and Conference Center. This camp is very much alive today and continues under the umbrella of the Canadian Sunday School Mission.

I became acquainted with the John Reimers in those early days and was so happy in more recent years to give them the story of how God helped us develop a Christian camp in Trinidad (see next chapter). John asked me if we could use the help of a group of men from his area. I thanked him for such a generous offer and invited them to visit Ridgewalk in Trinidad. He has come at various times and for the last eight years has spent up to eight weeks at a time. When not able to bring a group, he and Gwen come alone.

It is always a pleasant surprise to welcome, each year, a growing number of teams and work groups from Canada and the USA to help put Ridgewalk together. These people have given their time and finances to make Ridgewalk what it is today. Our hearts well up in praise to God that Christian camping plays a major role in the life of believers all over Trinidad.

A final happy note. Ness Lake campers save some of their "tuck" (canteen allowance) to send to the children of Ridgewalk Camp each year who have little for such purposes. Also, others at Ness Lake offset the cost of Trinidad campers who wouldn't have the funds to pay for a whole week at camp. They have contributed as much as $3,000 a year. No wonder that Ness Lake and Ridgewalk are known as sister camps. God blesses these volunteers as they go back to their homes spreading the good news of Christian camping in such places as Trinidad.

The Ben Penners, overseers of camp construction, receive service award from WT Dir., Albert Ehmann.

Ridgewalk Camp and Conference Centre

Ben's memorial plaque at camp

# 17
# Ridgewalk Camp Becomes a Reality

1956 was the year I discovered that camping could happen in Trinidad, and it could be fun. However, that first trial run meant sleeping on a sawdust bed in a tent, teaching in a bamboo patch, telling campers to go easy on the water as well as keeping a dozen girls happy and in line. When it came to sleeping, there were muffled giggles often late into the night. When we got up we discovered sawdust not only in our shoes but between our sheets. Around 10:00 a.m. each morning we welcomed that predictable cool breeze on our hilltop campus. Such was my introduction to camping with a tropical flavor. I was convinced that this island brand of Christian camping could stand plenty of improvement.

One Sunday afternoon we discovered a teenager from our Siparia congregation at our door. Hammid proudly produced a sketch of buildings for a camp set-up for which we had long been dreaming. "Here's a plan for a camp of our own," Hammid offered. I assured our young friend that I would stand behind him every step of the way. "But Hammid, you must take the lead." He smiled his approval. Reluctant at first to be on a camp committee, I found myself volunteering to help. No doubt about it, Christian camping in Trinidad turned out to be one of the most exciting involvements of my life.

The camp committee had a question for our church leaders. "If we purchase land for a camp, will you stand with us?" That question was met with a strong "Yes" from all the pastors. We began by asking the government to give us fifteen acres for a camp. Every request turned out to be futile. We felt we should trust the Lord for fifteen acres and that ten of them should be suitable for residences and five for agricultural use.

Can you imagine our joy when a piece of land was eventually found that met those requirements? This ideal fifteen acre piece in south Trinidad was designated for agriculture, and would have to be reclassified for use as a residential camp. Also we were told, "only one building would be allowed on the property." In two years some of the more severe restrictions the government wanted to put on us were lifted in answer to our prayers. After testing the soil, the government informed us that ten acres of this parcel was suitable for a residential camp and five acres for agricultural purposes. Within six months our churches had fully paid for the land. Our Good Shepherd was giving us the green light.

The morning of the dedication of the land my prayer partner and I took a faith walk and claimed the promise that God had given first to Moses centuries before, then to Joshua: *"Every place that the sole of your foot shall tread upon have I given you"* (Josh. 1:3). Our speaker that morning, David Crane from TEAM (The Evangelical Alliance Mission) underscored the responsibility that lay before us. "You now have land for a camp. But this will take much faith, prayer and fasting before you have a functioning camp here." Who would have dreamed that day that countless dozens of trips would have to be made to the water and electrical companies and that it would take seven years before electricity would be connected and nine before water would be hooked up. There were new lessons to learn as God taught us to wait on Him.

One day, with letter in hand, my prayer partner and I walked into the offices of one of three oil companies in Trinidad. In building the camp, we were told that we could use drill pipes, six inches wide and thirty feet long. The Public Relations Manager of one of these companies encouraged me by saying he could grant this request but that it would take time. In one of the many visits I was asked, "Miss Johnson, could you use some mattresses and bunks?" I told him that we most certainly could. We plan to have a residential camp I told him, that will hold one hundred persons. But what about the storage of this massive amount of mattresses and bunks? God had a big surprise for us. I viewed four large containers of equipment and now I was hearing the gentleman say, "Edith, you can have it all, but you will have to move quickly, so get your trucks and come back. ("What trucks?" I chuckled inwardly). The storage site must be safe, dry and with room to hold all the equipment."

Falteringly I asked the wife of the manager of the oil company, "Do you suppose, since we don't have any place to store this, that the oil company could find storage for us?" Within a half hour arrangements were made and when we returned several hours later, we followed a man who led us to a large bungalow where the inside walls had been removed. The friendly gentleman told us, "There will be no problem storing all your equipment in this bungalow." Not only was it going to be safe and dry there, it was within one block of my home.

As God provided one thing after another, we moved ahead. Perhaps the camp should have been called "Miracle Camp."

Next, one of our committee members asked, "Who can we get to take the oversight of building the camp?" We prayed, and we thought of a few possibilities, and scrapped half of them. Finally we agreed that no one seemed more suited to fill the bill than former missionaries, Ben and Marguerite Penner. One problem: the Penners were back in their home in Portland, Oregon, taking care of their aged mother. Would they be free to come to Trinidad? Marguerite's mother had been an amazing prayer partner for her Trinidadian children as well as for people all over the world. She had passed on to her reward. Ben had the necessary skills and a heart for hard work. This had been evident in the early years that the Penners had carried a heavy schedule in Trinidad. But would they return to take on this responsibility, especially as they too were getting up in years? All these questions were soon answered when their answer finally arrived. "Yes, we feel that we should take up the challenge." We learned that this response came only after diligently seeking the Lord.

Now a second question loomed like a mountain. Where do we get the money to start building? Yet the words had come to me so clearly, *"The best of the land of Egypt will be yours"* (Gen 45:18). Certainly a wonderful promise but how could it be worked out in a practical way?

I watched with admiration as the Penners literally threw themselves into the task of bringing this camp into being. We had to agree on a name so that we could use it in all our business transactions. Eventually the camp committee came up with "Ridgewalk Camp and Conference Center." This was to become not just a name but a spiritual mountaintop for thousands of people. I was convinced that our God again had given us the best when He gave us back this couple to develop the camp. Although I could not involve myself in the physical labor, God gave me the privilege of being part of almost every development at Ridgewalk.

As the years have passed, local people and many excellent work teams from North America, often sacrificing their own vacations, arrived at the Ridgewalk site to serve God with their gift of helps. They cleared land, they built cabins, cottages and dormitories, an all-purpose activities center that doubled for dining hall, kitchen and meeting room. A good-sized swimming pool and generous playground took shape and Ridgewalk was up and running. God allowed the Penners the joy of seeing a completed camp center before the Lord took Ben home. A memorial plaque at the Ridgewood Center today honors the Penners' faithful work.

A few months before the Penners left Trinidad, I asked who of our local people would fill the gap of leadership at the camp. Permission was given me to scout around for someone. I realized I had bitten off more than I could chew. My heart cried out, "Father, you've heard what I have said. Please, please lead me to Your choice."

A music retreat had just finished at the camp when a young man offered to carry my overhead projector. He had been one of the children who had attended Sunday School by the creek in Williamsville through the mentoring of Brother Tallboy. "Thanks," I told Vijay in parting, "I really appreciated your help." We both went our separate ways.

Do you want to hear the rest of the story? Vijay with his sweet wife Aloma eventually joined our camp team and served in the leadership of Ridgewalk for many fruitful years right up to the present. This team of two have done every imaginable thing to make the camp run smoothly, including the purchasing, cooking and serving of thousands of meals. These two kernels of wheat have offered their lives selflessly, and through their sacrifices and obedience to the Lord's call, have witnessed many a Trinidadian coming into the Kingdom of God. And when they retire, which is not too many years from now, God will have His replacements. After all is He not called Jehovah Jirah, "The Lord will provide?"

1962, the year Donna Williamson and I "teamed up."

# 18
# Friends, Coffee
# and a Bible Study

From where we lived in Marabella, Donna and I could look across at the mammoth Texaco Refinery (nationalized today as Petrotrin). The center of the oil industry on the island, it buzzed with activity in the day, and at night its lights flooded the whole refinery making it look like one massive Christmas tree. Added to that were the gigantic flames that stretched skyward, venting the excess gasses. Within this area were some 250 bungalows, most of them occupied by expatriate oil workers and their wives from the U.S. There were some "Trinnies" there as well.

Materially the oil workers from abroad seemed to have all they needed of this world's goods. Being somewhat of a self-contained group on the refinery, they had little need of interacting with their outside world, nor did most of them choose to. Neither did the Trinnies have reason to go inside the guarded gates, other than for their jobs at the refinery. Donna and I often wondered at the emptiness that must have characterized the lives of these expatriates. God burdened us for the many women who were almost prisoners of the Texaco refinery. There surely must be a way to break this social barrier to reach these isolated Americans. We wrestled with this problem; we tried to be innovative, and of course we prayed a good deal. The answer soon came and in a most interesting way.

I answered my phone that particular day and the gentleman calling had a definite Texan accent. Joe Kanewskie, an engineer from Groves, Texas on a two-year stint with Texaco in Trinidad, told us something we longed to hear. It looked very much like the answer to our prayers. Joe said that he and his wife Beverly were trying to find a good church and discovered that I was connected with a group of evangelical congregations. As I listened to his conversation, I was thinking that this was just the Christian connection we needed inside the refinery, Joe shared that the two of them were anxious to enjoy Christian fellowship on the outside. They, with son Robert, soon became our best friends.

Visiting Beverly one day, I asked, "Why don't you start a Bible class inside Texaco for the women that live here?"

"I have never taught a Bible class, and would be a little fearful to start," she told me. We were about to begin a Keswick Deeper Life Conference in Trinidad, so I asked Beverly if she would be willing to take in Dr. and Mrs. Stephen Olford, the speaker and his wife. The Kanewskies agreed and found the Olfords a delightful couple. But would you believe this, the Olfords put the same question to Beverly about starting a class with the women. Beverly in fear and trembling agreed to start one. Chuckling she confessed to me that the prayer she prayed before her first study, was, "Lord, please don't let anyone come to this class."

God used Beverly and her quiet but sincere teaching of the Bible for the remainder of her two years in Trinidad. Just before she left, she asked me, "Edith, will you take this class?" After praying about it and knowing that I could delegate to someone eventually, I told her I would pray about it. Shortly after, I overheard Beverly telling the women that I would be taking the class. I really needed that shove as the door that God opened at the refinery was the beginning of new life for many a woman there. After all, having a captive audience worked, and a number of lives were transformed.

When we saw the Lord at work in the lives of these Trinnies and ex-pats, we felt confident He wanted us to do something for the women of Trinidad both inside and outside of Texaco. So

I started another Bible class in a very needy section and Donna began two studies as well.

I realized that this ministry to women would never grow until it was led by locals. Further, we decided once it got into the hands of the locals, we would look for a source of training materials that they could handle. Having heard from a friend on the island of Barbados about introducing studies put out by Stonecroft and its success, we sent for samples. And were we able to find someone to take the leadership? Read on.

In one of the classes I was teaching, a young lady appeared with four other women.

Let me introduce one of them to you. Young and attractive, Margaret Harris was outgoing and vivacious. (Since that first meeting, she has had a surname change to Keeler[2]).

Margaret was eager to share her first impressions of life at that time and what the Bible classes meant to her. She says:

> "The Lord introduced me to these classes by a written invitation. At that stage in my life I was not in need financially, I was not in need socially, I already could be called a socialite, a real jet-setter. The written invitation said that Edith Johnson taught the Bible class and it had changed the writer's life. I had noticed a change in this woman, too. Yes, I had been given a brief personality sketch of Edith Johnson from my sister living in Barbados. She had done a course with Edith on Fulfilled Womanhood. She told me in her introduction of Edith, 'when she talks it is like God speaking.' My only recollection of people like that were those who wore long gowns and head pieces. So when she described this Miss Johnson teaching the class, I would have to go and see what she looked like and maybe even learn something about the Bible. So we went in and I saw a simple little lady sitting at one end of the room and other ladies around her and I thought 'I wonder where this Edith Johnson is?' I was expecting to see a lady with nothing less than a crown on her head wearing a flowing white gown who spoke like God. Then the little lady at the end of the room spoke. She said, 'Good afternoon, ladies, I am so glad

2    Richard and Margaret Keeler are active in an Evangelical Mennonite Church-planting ministry in Trinidad.

to see all of you today.' What! Surely this wasn't the lady that my sister had spoken about."

"When I got home, I had been given a tag with Edith's name on it, and a Bible. I put the Bible on the shelf and threw the name tag in a drawer of nuts, bolts and screws, and now and again I would go into the drawer to look for something and would prick my finger on the name tag. Edith Johnson and my sister would come to mind and what she said about the lady that spoke like God. As I continued to go back to these studies, I listened intently to her comments concerning Jesus being born of a virgin, something I could never accept. Then using Genesis 3, verse 15, she explained about God speaking to Satan telling him that because he had tempted Eve and she had chosen to sin, that one day God would send His Son, Jesus, through birth to a virgin, and that His Son would crush Satan's head. That spoke to me so loudly that I could hardly hear anything else. That was exactly where I was hung up."

I will always remember the third class we had. We were in Margaret's home and she prayed to have the Lord Jesus as resident in her heart. The Lord had brought this much younger woman into my life, just as the lady with the broad-brimmed hat, Ruby, had come into my life.

Margaret and I began to meet every week to study and pray together. She was a healthy baby! And by the way, she asked whether she could be a prayer partner with me just as Ruby had done. In fact, it was soon after that we named ourselves "the three musketeers." And by the way, Margaret eventually agreed to lead the Friendship Bible Classes. It happened this way.

I decided to call the ladies who were leading the classes to ask if any of them had someone in mind that they felt would consider becoming the leader. "I want to step back and let that person take over," I told them. What happened at this juncture was Margaret had to return to Scotland where she had five children still living in the home. She didn't think she could lead with the circumstances as they were, but would reconsider at a later time. In a matter of six months, all of her children were out of the home. God had cleared the way for her to come back to Trinidad. She added that after much prayer, she believed God would have her take responsibility for the Stonecroft Bible Classes. Now we had a Trinidadian-born leader who was willing to be trained as a coordinator of the classes. For me it was another budding friendship that was to grow. Because of Margaret's social background, she has touched many who would never otherwise have been reached for the Lord. God is using her today to start new classes so that almost every area of Trinidad and Tobago have Bible-based Stonecroft classes.

One thing in particular has blessed me about Margaret and her husband Richard; they have provided an apartment for me on the main floor of their home in Couva—for as long as I live. What an amazing provision! And it's good to know that I have them as close neighbors when needs and emergencies arise.

Would you believe that, beside the 30 Stonecroft leaders at the present, some of our ex-pats have started Bible classes in other parts of the world. Bless the Lord for these home ministries that reach out to those who won't normally darken the doors of a church, that transcend denominational barriers and truly bring these lost sheep into God's fold.

Edith and Donna

# 19
# Mischievous Memories

A favorite vacation spot that the missionaries in Trinidad used to enjoy was the beach house. This was one of the projects of missionary Ben Penner in his early years in Trinidad. The beach house, though rustic and simple in design, was on the ocean, and that filled the bill for Donna and me. It might not pass the building code on a beach in my home state, but it was a great escape from the busyness of life in Trinidad.

This was also an ideal place for newlyweds who didn't have the means to go to touristy places outside the island. One couple, we will call Hector and Liz, had met each other in Trinidad and had each finished Bible College. They were very excited about what the Lord had in store for them together as pastoring couple to their own people. Hector was a serious-minded student type while Liz was more outgoing and fun.

Certain missionaries were delighted to help them get to the beach house for a short honeymoon. Dare I mention that Donna and I and missionaries such as Clifford and Reathel Gross and their four young children made up the select group that were to drive Hector and Liz to the beach house, since they didn't have a car of their own. I was driving my dream car (chapter 9), while the happily married couple were riding with the Grosses and their children. After viewing a special site along the way, Liz jumped back into the Grosses car expecting them to wait for Hector. But no, the secret orders were for them to take off with the bride while the single women would make sure that bashful Hector would ride with them. So, squeezed in between these singles, Hector became puzzled at first at what was happening. And when the ladies felt he should do some sightseeing with them, he was not amused. After a good hour along the route, it began to get a little dusk. The lagging carload of singles and one non-talking groom; finally arrived at the beach house.

Since the Grosses had gotten there first, Reathel had pulled out the kids' pajamas and was getting the younger set ready for the night. You mean they were going to stay overnight? Well at least that's what the newly-weds had been told after arriving at the beach house. And it was also said that in the dark it just might not be wise to travel the lonely road back before daylight. A very crestfallen Hector was beside himself. Wouldn't you be if you were in his shoes?

After a few minutes in the holiday house, where most of the attendants were making merry, I finally said, "Maybe we should go home. It would be hard for all of us to sleep here. We should give you two (speaking to the new bride and groom), the run of the place." What relief came over the faces of Hector and Liz. As we said our good byes and wished them well, Liz laughingly nodded her approval to our misdeeds while Hector seemed pleased that they would be alone at last.

This couple spent some fruitful years as they pastored a church in Trinidad, in spite of the rough beginnings, thanks to those pranksters.

Moral of this true story: don't under-estimate the extent to which "seasoned" missionaries and their cohorts can tease the innocent, and unsuspecting.

# 20
# Furnished and Free

I was facing yet another move. I had lived a whole year in the lovely home that had come to us through those mysterious phone calls. But Donna was returning to the U.S. and with the coming of a new missionary couple, Hugh and Sylvia Foshee, I felt keenly that God wanted me to give up this place. Ruby, my prayer partner, argued, "You know how hard it was to find. Where are you going?"

"That's true," I replied. "I really believe that I should give the incoming missionary family this nice clean house." I hadn't an inkling where I would live. I had loved this home and had lived in it for a whole year. Was this blind faith on my part? The battle was fierce and given my prayer partner's feelings about it, I found myself often in tears.

I particularly recall the Sunday morning with tears running down my face, I told the Lord, "I will obey You and give up the house." But I did remind Him that I had no place to go. That was about 6:00 a.m. Then at 6:30 a.m. the same morning, my prayer partner stepped inside the door, put her arms around me and said, "Edith, you have to give up the house." Somewhat surprised at her change of attitude, I told her that I had already done that. I'm sure this was the confirmation I needed. God was in control, He would work it out.

Hugh and Sylvia Foshee had been reticent to take up my offer, but finally gave in. So I moved to Tony and Gwen's bungalow on the Texaco Oil property. Gwen had asked me to stay in their home for three months while they visited England. That gave me one whole day to move all my stuff. Could I do it?

Ruby had asked that I stay at her house that evening. When I got to Ruby's, however, she had fallen and had been taken to emergency. I rushed to the hospital, took hold of Ruby's hand and told her to squeeze it if she heard me. There was no response so I cried out to the Lord to intervene. I later found out she had broken her neck and would be in cast for a long time.

I finally moved all my things to my temporary quarters on the Texaco property. When it came time for Ruby to be released, her husband Franklin had suffered a massive stroke. With their four children in school they wondered what they should do. I suggested that Ruby come and recuperate at my place. I thought that might be ten days or so. Four months passed before she was able to move back to her own place.

Living now at my place, Ruby often used her recuperation time to pray. One day as she stood looking out the window at the oil refinery property, she called to her Father, "O God, I see a bungalow over there that is empty. Now, I don't know how You will do it, but would You please make it possible for Edith to live there? She doesn't have any place to go after she leaves here. Please grant this request." When I came home that night, Ruby shared what she had told the Lord. "This can never happen," I told her, "You know that people get on the property only by invitation."

"Yes, but I told the Lord about it and I truly believe that God wants it to happen."

Then she went on talking, "I need your help. You must write a letter and you get everybody in the Bible classes to sign it and we'll send it to the Bungalow Committee and ask them for permission to live in this empty bungalow." So the ladies agreed that we were holding onto Ruby's faith by her coat-tail because we thought it was foolish to even think of doing this. However, the letter was written. I was amazed how they had gotten the details of my life. They signed the letter and submitted it to the committee. A response finally arrived. "We are sorry but at this point we do not have a place that is suitable for Edith Johnson."

It seemed we had come to a dead end.

The day came when Ruby felt she was ready to go back to her own home. At the same time, the Lord put it on my heart to go to my home in Washington State. How I bless the Lord for His timing—three weeks after my arrival I was to witness the passing of my dear father. Mother assured me, that with daughters living near by, I should go back to my work in Trinidad.

After staying six months in Ruby's home, one of the ladies from the Bible class talked to the man in charge of the bunga-lows. He casually told her that my request had been put in file 13. So she said to him, "We don't want that to be the end. See if you can pull it up again." So Mr. Matthews began a bit of politicking. He knew the men that opposed me, that didn't want me there because I taught a Bible class. So when Mr. Matthews went to the general manager, a Christian man, he told Matthews to bring the matter up again at counsel meeting. Almost two days later, I had a letter from the oil company. "We have now found a place that would be suitable for you. We will clean it up and paint it and we will make any minor changes."

To me that place looked palatial after having no place of my own for some months. Different friends helped me move all my belongings to the refurbished bungalow. I lived almost like a queen in that beautiful place for 21 years! That's the lon-gest that I stayed in any one house in Trinidad. *This God is our God for ever and ever. He will be my guide even unto death"* (Ps. 48:14). I did not pay for electricity. I did not pay for gas. If anything went wrong with any of the appliances, all I needed to do was pick up the phone and call. I learned once more that giving up things for the Lord, always has a pay back day. God is no man's debtor.

Texaco bungalow

Texaco bungalow—First phase on the way up.

# 21
# Vicious Attack

In the bungalow on the now nationalized Texaco property, all was quiet where I slept, except for the occasional croak of a frog in the nearby slough. I had asked the Lord to keep me safe as I slept. About 3:30 in the morning, that quietness was broken by a sudden shuffling of feet, then a thud as a man landed on top of me. A raucous voice announced " I'm going to rape you, I'm going to rape you." This Trinidadian had grabbed my bath towel from the shower so he could muzzle me. To my horror, I felt the edge of a cutlass blade on my back. Every time I moved my head just enough to get a gasp of air, I cried out, "Lord Jesus, help me. Lord help me." This only provoked the man and he pounded me harder. Living in a duplex, I hoped Sherry, the lady next door, would hear my cries. At first she thought I was having a heart attack. "I will call security," she had said to herself. Suddenly my neighbour heard the thump of the two of us landing on the floor. "You must come right away," Sherry urged security over the phone. "My neighbour is being attacked."

When the security guards arrived my assailant quickly let go of me. He called to me to give him all the money (around $50 US). I told him he could have anything in the house but leave me alone. He grabbed the money and ran. It was then I found I was in shock. I didn't get a look at my attacker but knew that he wore a cap and that he was naked (Often those who threaten a sexual attack grease their bodies so that they can easily slip from their victim's grasp.) God seemed to give me super human strength to free myself, not allowing the man to fulfill his evil intentions. At the back door he picked up some of his things, heard someone coming and dropped them and ran. Mounting the fence, he was nabbed by a guard. "I got him and I know where these fellows run," the guard announced as he returned. "I put a gun in his mouth and told him if he resisted he was a dead man. He's in the van and security officers have their feet on him."

Twice I asked the guard whether he would allow me to talk to the man. "Why do you ever want to talk to that man?"

"That man is making wrong choices in life and I want to explain to him that Jesus Christ loves him and can change him." Finally I realized though, with men having their feet placed firmly on his body he would hardly be in the frame of mind to listen to the Gospel or anything else I might say.

In the meantime, neighbors had gathered to find out why all the commotion. One of the nuns who lived in a nearby bungalow talked face to face with the man. She asked him, "Why did you do that? That was a very bad thing for you to do. Tell me, why did you try to assault this woman?"

After a pause, he confessed, "They put a light on me and I had to do it." Immediately I knew that this was an attack prompted by witchcraft. The poor man was under the power of demons, and they had instructed him to do this. One of the police women looked at me and said, "I have never known a lady of your age who has come through an experience like you have who has lived to tell the story." I was glad I could tell her that it was because of my heavenly Father. My neighbor encouraged me when she said to those present, "It's her strong faith in God that enabled her to handle it the way she did."

"We are going to take you to the hospital on the grounds and have you checked," the police offered. Shelly asked if she might go along. We stopped at the security offices where Shelly faced my assailant. He was sitting on a bench with his head bowed. "I could have wrung his neck," she scolded. Next we were taken to the San Fernando Hospital where I was checked more thoroughly. After giving me some tablets, the doctor told me to go home and relax, "You need to be quiet." Although a good suggestion, he missed the point a bit. Little did he understand that when you belong to God's family, you are not alone, nor is being alone always the answer. At least fifty of my beloved Trinidadians visited. What an outpouring of love!

As soon as Ken Ragonath, one of the island's respected Christian leaders heard about my encounter, he came to see me. "Edith, I have come to apologize on behalf of the men of Trinidad. You left your home country and came here only to do us good. And this is how we have repaid you." I looked Ken in the eye and said, "This does not change my opinion about men in Trinidad one bit. This was only one man and I'm convinced he doesn't represent the majority of men on the island." Many times I have thanked the Lord for this godly young man who brought me such encouragement that day.

Without realizing it, I discovered that God was putting my need on the hearts of people in various parts of the world and in particular, three felt the Lord nudging them to pray for me.

Margaret Keeler, Ruby Thompson and I.
(Dubbed "The 3 Musketeers")

# 22
# Three Intercessors

I hadn't fully recovered from the vicious attack. I was told that I should go back to my home in the USA. It seemed that God in His wisdom was pointing me in that direction. But, I wondered, when my Trinidadian friends are attacked where can they go? Two World Team leaders who were in Trinidad for a seminar urged me to get away from my work. They told me, "The trauma from an experience like this can last several months. In fact, " they said, "there is little difference from what our soldiers expressed in Viet Nam." In that case, I promised, I would go.

The very day I arrived back in the U.S., I had to deal with flashbacks. The Mission's counsellor who picked me up at the airport had to run on a short errand. I stayed in the vehicle and suddenly two men appeared. I froze. A few days later I experienced a second flashback. A worker was cleaning our yard, minding his own business, but I was sure he was there to attack me. Again, I froze. Right then I said to the Lord, "I can't go on like this. I am not the servant of fear. I am your servant. O God, please come to my aid."

Finally the day came when I was allowed to return to Trinidad. I would be going back to the very same bungalow where my nightmare occurred. A dear friend from the Bible Coffee Fellowship was on hand to encourage me. "We are going to see that your apartment is made secure. We will help pay for burglar bars for the windows and doors and this will make your place safer." I rejoiced and thanked her for this kindness. There was another thing I found that helped me. Every time I came back home again through the oil company's gated entrance, I would pray at the top of my voice, "Lord, I am your servant. I am not the servant of fear. You gave the promise, *"Fear not."* I'd quote every Scripture I could think of that had to do with fear. In my devotions one morning God affirmed to me by giving the promise, *"After you have suffered a while, I am going to restore you."* Oh, how I hung on to that verse—it was God's strong word to me.

About a year after the attack, Dean Franklin, World Team Director for the Caribbean at that time, asked me, "Edith, how are you really doing?" I rejoiced to tell him of the glory of God, "I'm doing just fine, really and truly."

One of the most valuable lessons I learned during and after the attack was how God intervenes when people pray. I found that people all over the world were praying for me during those crisis days. Three people stood out in particular.

A year before the attack I met a man by the name of Joe Knoblauch who was driving his car for his sister in Philadelphia. He didn't care to drive in the big city, but as he learned about my life in Trinidad, he promised that he would pray daily for my physical safety, asking the Lord to watch over me. He said that it wasn't until after he heard what happened, that the burden lifted.

Then one of my prayer partners whom I introduced to you earlier, Margaret, was in Scotland at the time. She called and told me, "One day recently, while I was trying to have my quiet time, all I could think of was you. I said to myself, 'I guess I will just stop and pray for Edith.'" I found out that was the very day I was being attacked. How I praise the Lord for putting this burden on Margaret's heart.

But this is not all. My other prayer partner, Ruby, who was in the U.S. at the time, had a strange dream that very night. She dreamt that "a lady of the cloth" was attacked. Here's how she described it:

"I immediately woke up thinking that this mysterious person must have been my sister who was an inspector in home economics in the school system. So I called her and told her about my strange dream. Please be careful, I warned her, because the lady of the cloth in my dream was attacked."

It wasn't long after that Ruby learned it was I who had been attacked. It was then it all came together. God was saying to her that she had to pray for "the lady of the cloth." I pass this on to you, not so much for the experience itself, but for the lessons God has taught me about God's work through believing prayer. In every circumstance He is in control.

Learning that my attacker was to do nine years in prison, I sensed the Lord was now giving me the opportunity to write him a letter. I assured this man that I had completely forgiven him. Next, I pointed him to Jesus. I never did hear from him but maybe to my delight, I will meet this man in heaven, redeemed as a brother in Christ.

Teaching the young.

# 23
# Lord, Teach Me to Pray

To know that God holds His great umbrella over us, as in the "vicious attack," and to see that He uses His servants to bind the enemy, is strengthening to say the least. I have had a lifetime of learning in God's school room. I would be the first to say that I have not yet arrived, but I constantly carry deep within my heart the fervent desire, "Lord, teach me to pray."

Allow me to share the following eight aspects of prayer— just a few truths that God has taught me over the years.

## 1. The Lord can and will supply my every need.

*"But my God will meet all your needs according to his glorious riches in Christ Jesus"* (Phil 4:19). Since it was not the Lord's will to give me a husband, He began to impress upon me that He wanted to fulfill that role in my life. I had to prove the reality of what I had said many times to others. I realized that my part was to sit at Jesus' feet and to allow His Holy Spirit to instruct me in every area of my life. So often I have prayed, "Lord, I want to know You in a deep, intimate way as my Father, my Saviour, my indwelling Holy Spirit. Please develop this aspect of my life." He is doing more than what He promised.

## 2. I must have a deep hunger for God's Word.

*"I have hidden your word in my heart that I might not sin against you"* (Ps. 119:11). This hunger started in my early years. I could hardly wait to get alone with the Lord and His Word—such

was my hunger. As the Scriptures became more powerful in my heart, the importance of prayer likewise grew. It also put up a strong barrier against sin and temptation.

## 3. Use Shorter Portions of Scripture.

"Don't feel you have to read several chapters in the Bible each day." That advice was good news to me. The Lord may want you to meditate and chew on a verse or two, and do it thoroughly. I began to do that as I would get on my knees before the Lord. The Holy Spirit showed me how beneficial that approach can be. Often, from one verse or two, the Lord would direct me in how to pray for others and myself for that day, or for the special need that faced me right then.

## 4. Good books can often give help in effective praying.

Using my love of good books, the Holy Spirit showed me how men and women of God, older saints as well as contemporary writers, could sharpen my prayer focus. These "knew their God" through the path of the Word and prayer.

One who made a tremendous impact on my life and I feel has often mentored me is Amy Carmichael. In hours of great need in my walk, God chose to place deep within my heart, lessons that He had taught her. Prayer was like breathing to her. Often, after reading her books, I would pray, "Father, please do that same work in me." Memorizing some of the lessons she had learned and expressed in the form of poetry, became a part of my expressions of prayer.

As recently as May 2008, when my committee was planning for the ministry of a group of women from British Columbia I suggested that each time we met, we pray this prayer together:

THINK THROUGH ME

Think through me, thoughts of God,
My Father, quiet me,
'Till in Thy holy presence, hushed
I think Thy thoughts with Thee.

Think through me, thoughts of God,
That always everywhere,
The stream that through my being flows
May homeward pass in prayer.

Think through me, thoughts of God,
And let my own thoughts be
Lost like the sand-pools on the shore
Of Thy eternal sea.

—Amy Carmichael

Even now as I read these lines, they come to me afresh and create a burning in my heart. So, do not overlook what saints of old, and God's people today, have written.

## 5. Keep a Prayer Journal.

This is another suggestion I would give you, which I wish I had done in former years. Keep a journal of what God is saying to you as well as what you are telling Him. Then go back once in a while and read it. It could bring refreshing as you see what you once promised God and what He has since done for you.

## 6. Try Different Postures in Prayer.

Sometimes you will feel like responding to God by prostrating yourself on the floor. Often this has seemed the only appropriate thing to do, the only proper place to be. At times it seemed the Lord spoke audibly to me. He was teaching me more and more that He indeed is a Father to me, and a Husband that I could count on. Often as I walk, I find it easy to pour out my heart to God especially if I find myself in some great need.

For example, one day I was walking through the Trinidad airport. I didn't have enough money to hire a taxi to take me to my parked car in Trincity. I reminded my Father that I desperately needed His care. I told Him that no responsible father would leave His child without taking care of her. Right then the Lord assured me that He had gone before. I walked out of the airport to find a vehicle waiting to take me to my car. God had abundantly answered.

## 7. Work on your Praise Life.

My prayer life was growing, but I discovered that my praise life was stunted. God used Ruby Thompson, my prayer partner, to show me this. So often I would hear her praise audibly, "Thank You, Father, O thank You, Father." She was a woman who had faith to believe the unthinkable, and what seemed the unattainable. She often saw her prayers answered, in most cases, without much delay. Thanksgiving was always her spontaneous response. Not surprising, really. The Scriptures tell us that *"God dwells in the praises of His people."*

There's a wonderful event that happens here in Trinidad among believers. When God does something special—raising up a sick person, providing a new home, blessing a couple getting married, it gives the Trinidadians a reason to hold a Thanksgiving event where they invite people to come and rejoice with them. This Thanksgiving celebration is not limited to a special day like we have in North America; it can happen any time of the year. It's a jubilee of thanks directing much praise and glory to God.

## 8. Prayer and the Great Commission

One more thing about prayer is that you cannot separate prayer from missions. Interceding for others in the world at large became more and more a part of my life as the years went by. Bit by bit God began to show me that the reason His people in the South Eastern Caribbean were not praying effectively for missionaries and the nations of the world, was because we were not showing them how to pray for this kind of outreach. Much information was coming into my hands about the whole aspect of global missions and about the persecuted church, but we were not challenging believers in our islands to take up the torch and run with it.

These are just eight brief things that I am learning in God's school of prayer. There's so much more to learn from Scripture and from those who have gone before us.

"Lord, help me, help us all to delight in spending more time with You, listening to Your voice and interceding more effectively on behalf of others."

# 24
# Advancing
## Three More Villages Open their Doors

I had the privilege in mid-1979 of joining a brand new team. On this team I welcomed Siddhant and Beulah Yogi, already serving in Trinidad with World Team. Originally they had come from India with another couple, the Emmanuel Endigeris. The Endigeris are involved in a thriving work among Indians in a more central area of Trinidad. Another couple, Irwin and Aggie Klassen from northern Alberta, joined us for a two-year term. The team was truly international. Our joint ministry gave us access to three new areas, Barrakpore, Palmiste and Borde Narve.

Although we were a brand new team, none of us were novices. We each had some years of experience in the Lord's work. Not surprisingly, we differed in methodology. What an opportunity to learn to appreciate one another and you can be sure there were countless times that we had to work hard to be a team.

Would you like to know one particular thing I learned? There is not necessarily a right and a wrong way to accomplish a certain task, but there may be a different way. I found there was a desperate need to make room for the other person without feeling threatened. I, as a single person, saw the need to have a positive attitude when I was not given what I felt was my rightful place. Submission to God-given authority was certainly needed at times. I realized that when east meets west there will always be a difference, but to learn to handle these in a godly manner and not to back off from the others involved, is a valuable, valuable lesson. Another lesson was to see this as a growing opportunity and not a negative thing. As I reflect on this experience, my heart is filled with thanksgiving for each of these, my colleagues.

At the beginning of the Barrackpore work, the Klassens had a unique role. Most of the people were of East Indian background and were strong in their belief system. The Klassens had drawn up a realistic approach for reaching these people with something like a correspondence course, Irwin and Aggie would go into a home and ask for a commitment from the whole family to study a prescribed lesson based on Scripture. A week later they would return to the home and check over the lesson that the family had worked on together. The Lord used this to open many doors and to lay a firm foundation for the work in the particular village. We also discovered strong opposition.

After our initial entrance into these three villages, a women's Bible class was in session, when a boy with the nickname of Scrapper came running. At the top of his voice he was shouting, "Pa dead in de garden; Pa dead in de garden!" All at the Bible class were related to Pa in one way or another, and all raced to where Pa was lying. One could have called this scenario "The case of the vanishing Bible class." It seems a heart attack had taken Pa's life. This poor soul had violently opposed those who were bringing in this "new" teaching to his village. Though as far as we knew he had made no confession of faith in Jesus, in time every one of his family, including his wife, trusted Jesus for salvation.

We know that God is not finished with what He wants to do in Palmiste, Barrackpore and Borde Narve. Without question, as a new team we sensed that when God opens doors this wide, no man can shut them.

## To the Ends of the Earth.

Another milestone occurred in taking the Great Commission beyond the coastlines of Trinidad and Tobago. As a group we formed what we called "Advance International." God had raised up 55 churches throughout the English-speaking islands of the South Eastern Caribbean since 1949. These churches stretched down the chain of islands from St. Lucia to Trinidad and are all members of the national organization that was initiated by World Team. Under ECWI (Evangelical Church of the West Indies), many hundreds of people in this island chain are singing God's praises and seeing neighbors and friends brought into the family of God. But this is not where the movement ends.

Over the years a number of us had a growing desire to send young people to other islands and countries as well as to back them in prayer. Out of this vision, and with the help of World Team, Advance International was the ideal vehicle to send abroad nationals from local West Indian congregations. The church in St. Lucia was the first to model this outreach in 1986 when they sent Nazaire and Maryann George to French Guiana to establish a church. This couple retired in 2007, but they continue to assist in the church there and are beginning a new work in French Guiana. I felt honored to serve on Advance International as Prayer Coordinator and have the joy of reporting what God is doing in other countries. For several years regular prayer reports have been circulating and we trust all our churches will eventually become a vibrant part of this intercessory outreach. Happily I was able to turn my prayer leadership over to Edris Marks from the island of Grenada, a former worker with Operation Mobilization. Each November we have a Prayer Retreat using letters and prayer folders from World Team. Please ask God to empower those involved in this major task.

An effective evangelistic thrust known as T &T for Jesus, simply standing for Trinidad & Tobago for Jesus, is a recent outreach to the people of our two islands. My good friend Heather Olford spoke highly of an evangelist by the name of David Ford whom God was using in revival meetings in the USA and overseas. After visiting Mr. Ford, I asked him, "Would you be willing to spend some weeks in an evangelistic effort in Trinidad?" At the invitation of the Keswick Committee in Trinidad, David came for the month of September, 2006. That was the launching of T & T For Jesus and Mr. Ford has returned each September. Many a life has been touched by God in salvation, revival and re-commitment.

This is particularly good news for the two islands of Trinidad and Tobago. Like many other parts of our world today, we hear daily reports of drug busts, kidnappings and thievery due to the lack of jobs. This often leads to suicides and other untimely deaths. Oh that God would bring a refreshing to all our churches and salvation to our beloved islanders.

## What Next?

I have just entered my 81st year. I am convinced that in the days ahead, the church here in Trinidad and Tobago will lift high the slogan, ADVANCING! The enemy will try his best to make us rest on our laurels. But God's Word leaves His soldiers no option. It's "forward march, no looking back!"

*Jan 3/14*

# EPILOGUE

Edith Johnson has lived life to the full in Trinidad for some 54 years. She's been given a lower floor apartment with two gracious missionaries, Margaret and Richard Keeler. Is this her earthly dwelling place until the Lord takes her home? You be the judge. Turn her loose on the colloquial Trinidadian English and she can rattle it off like the best of them. Ask her about spending her latter years in the island nation of Trinidad & Tobago and she'll answer with a big smile, "This is my home, these are my people."

In August of 2008, Edith passed a milestone—her 80th year. The Royal Hotel Banquet Room in Port of Spain, was beautifully decorated for the celebration. Everyone was in their finery and Edith was no exception. After some tributes and a special musical number, the audience was told that two special guests had arrived.

"Edith, would you please stand up?" Edith dutifully obeyed the emcee. "Now, turn around." There were two women, faces beaming, and a gasp of excitement burst from Edith. Lois and Marj, Edith's two sisters had come all the way from Washington State to share their younger sister's 80th birthday celebration. They had never before set foot on Trinidadian soil. Hugs, kisses and hearty clapping took place as the crowd watched the Johnson sisters embrace. Only one of the Johnson siblings hadn't yet made it to Trinidad, younger brother Roger. But he vowed he'd visit Edith one day in her island home.

So you think Edith will settle back and relax for a few months? No, not if you know Edith or have read this story thus far. As long as she has the strength and ability, she will delight in all that the Lord has ahead for her: traveling, speaking, visiting, listening, and as an octogenarian, she may just rest a little more often.

Thank you, Edith. We could use more kernels like you, buried in this world's soil, dying that others might live eternally.

# APPENDIX A

## What is World Team?

World Team traces its early beginnings to Elmer Thompson, a Colorado rancher turned missionary and B.G. Lavastida, a Cuban Presbyterian evangelist. These two men together in 1928 sought to evangelize the lost and to train disciples in Cuba. In time, this vision spread throughout the Caribbean Islands, South America and Europe. The early missionaries pioneered in planting churches and training national partners.

In the early 1990's World Team and other small-to-medium-sized mission agencies, with diminishing new recruits and tighter finances, struggled to stay afloat. Aggressive solutions were needed. World Team and Regions Beyond Missionary Union explored merger possibilities and officially joined hands in 1995 after much prayer and consultation between the leaders of both missions. As a result, World Team is world-wide in scope. Since blending the resources into the newly-formed World Team there has been a new focus on unevangelized people groups, forming national partnerships and emphasizing church multiplication.

During the 1950s, a number of church planters were called of God to the English-speaking islands, including Trinidad and Tobago. Among those was a single lady by the name of Edith Johnson. Those of us who served with her have been influenced by her love for people and by her identification with the culture. Edith's passion is planting churches, and she does it by making disciples. These disciples are scattered throughout Trinidad and Tobago. They have learned from her about prayer and dependence on the Lord. We salute and honor Edith, as she continues to serve and give glory to God.

Dean Franklin
former WT Director for the Caribbean

# World Team Roster
## of all those who have served in Trinidad/Tobago.

We want to honor and recognize the World Team missionaries who have served in the islands of Trinidad and Tobago since the beginning of the work in 1951. These have been co-laborers with Edith Johnson, even though often living far from each other. God has used the gifting of these and a good number of national pastors, their wives and Christian workers, in bringing people into the Kingdom. To God be all the glory! (We have arranged these in alphabetical order to facilitate the finding of any you may know.. An asterisk denotes persons who have gone to their heavenly reward. If you know of someone not on this list, tell us so that we can include them in a future print run.)

Auguiste, Muriel* (Hayne)
Bears, Regina*
Brunner, Joe and Lorene
Blyden, Roy and Gwen
Cross, Lloyd* and Anne*
Davis, Jack and Loretta
Dollar, Harold and Sharon
Dooknie, Ramdehal* and Nancy
Driskell, Billy and Pat
Endigeri, Immanuel and Sucheta
Fehr, Norman and Mary
Foshee, Hugh and Sylvia
Franklin, Dean and Edith

Gross, Cliff and Reathel
Grymaloski, Walt and Anne
Harms, Art* and Marg
Heppner, Mary*
Inglis, Donna (Williamson)
(Johnson, Edith)
Leavitt, Ray and Betty
Martinez, Joanne (Jackson)
Olbrich, Berthal and Sonja
Penner, Ben* and Marguerite
Peters, Harold* and Hazel
Plett, Mr and Mrs Don
Smith, LaVern and Marlene
Weber, Martin and Edna*
Wester, Bessie (Gingrich)
Whitermore, David and Marion
Yogi, Siddhant and Beulah
Zwaig, Mr and Mrs Bob

**<u>School Teachers</u>**
Merla Dick
Wilma Gibble
Helen Latham
Ginny Nelson
Ruth Phipps
Martha Sweeney

# APPENDIX B

## What is the ECWI?

The ECWI in Trinidad and Tobago came into being in 1951 under the leadership of Rev. Lloyd Cross, missionary of the West Indies Mission (known today as World Team). All the English-speaking island churches of the South Eastern Caribbean operate today as members of the ECWI (The Evangelical Church of the West Indies). These include St. Lucia, St. Vincent, Grenada, the Grenadines, and Trinidad and Tobago. In 1951 there were only seven ECWI churches in Trinidad and Tobago. Today there are sixteen, one of which is in Tobago.

The ECWI in Trinidad & Tobago has additional ministries geared to the various age groups such as Ridgewalk Camp & Conference Center (see Chapter 17) with a year-round ministry to all ages. We also have a training program, the Evangelical Institute of Christian Education (EICE) where we seek to train emerging leaders as well as the personnel involved in our Mission focus called Advance International (A.I.) (see chapter 24).

We have a five-year plan that includes doubling our present membership in our churches, planting three new churches, sending out five short term mission teams and five local teams, plus other worthy goals.

It is our vision to have all members committed to loving God, each other and all peoples both locally and cross-culturally. Our Mission is to glorify God by being a Christ-centered, Bible-based reproducing group of churches that fosters godly family life, strong discipleship, leadership, and outreach ministries.

* * * * * *

Edith Johnson, in her more than fifty-four years of service, has contributed significantly in most, if not all of the above. She, in collaboration with others, has planted six churches, and has discipled many of our present leaders, myself included (see Chapter 8).

We are extremely grateful to God for having sent her our way and for the ministry that she had and continues to have among us. It is our prayer that with God's help, she will continue to enjoy good health and be a blessing to all to whom she ministers directly and indirectly.

Rev. Michael Grant
Moderator, ECWI

# APPENDIX C

## Snapshot of Trinidad & Tobago

**Discovered:** by Christopher Columbus on his third voyage in 1498. Prior to this, tribes from South America, chiefly Arawaks and Caribs lived on these islands of the West Indies.

**Location:** Southeast Caribbean just 7 miles off the coast of Venezuela, South America.

**Combined Land Area:** 1,980 square miles (5,128 square km.)

**Population:** 1,300,500

**Climate:** Tropical

**Capitals:** Port of Spain, Trinidad; Scarborough, Tobago

**Official Language:** English

**Religions:** Roman Catholicism, Hinduism, Islam, Protestantism (main line as well as evangelical groups are 10% of population).

**Politics:** Trinidad & Tobago is a two-party republic. The Head of State of the two islands is the President, currently George Richards. The Head of Government is the Prime Minister, Patrick Manning. On August 31, 1962 Trinidad & Tobago became a nation independent from the United Kingdom and became a republic in 1976.

## Interesting Facts:

- **The first oil well** (actually the first in the world) was drilled in 1857, but full-fledged oil production was not underway until 1936 when Trinidad became the leading oil producer for the British Empire.

- **Crusoe's Cave** on Tobago's south coast fittingly memorializes Daniel Defoe's fictional adventurer, Robinson Crusoe.

- **The Pitch Lake** in Trinidad (see Chapter 8) has produced asphalt for centuries for the construction of roadways as well as other island needs. Only minimal lowering of the lake has taken place over the years.

- **Emancipation Day**, observed each August 1st since 1834, is the day that African slaves after more than 300 years in bondage, were freed. Street parades in traditional African dress, and displays of African history and culture, are part of the celebration.

- **Included** in Trinidad and Tobago's area, are 21 smaller islands.

- **The Steelband** originated in Port of Spain in the late 1930s. Indented pans, originally made from oil drums, are said to be the only musical instruments invented in the 20th century. The more modern steel pan today has become a highly sophisticated instrument capable of playing everything from classical to jazz, from gospel and hymns to the popular and catchy calypso tunes.

The adjoining map shows the listing of each Evangelical Church of the West Indies congregations, 16 in all.

# Trinidad & Tobago—One Nation

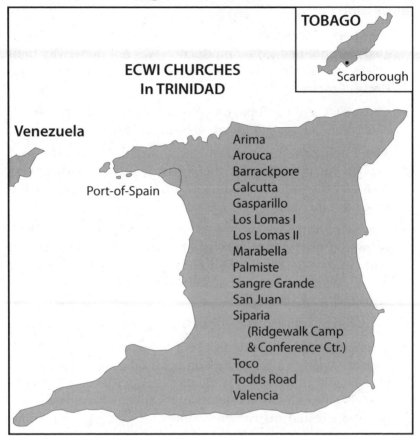

**TOBAGO**

Scarborough

**ECWI CHURCHES In TRINIDAD**

Venezuela

Port-of-Spain

Arima
Arouca
Barrackpore
Calcutta
Gasparillo
Los Lomas I
Los Lomas II
Marabella
Palmiste
Sangre Grande
San Juan
Siparia
    (Ridgewalk Camp
    & Conference Ctr.)
Toco
Todds Road
Valencia

---

**TO ORDER:** *TRINIDAD—My Home—My People*
use these addresses:

**CANADA:**
E-mail: mdinglis@shaw.ca
Mail:    12-3384 Gladwin,
           Abbotsford, BC
           V2S 7C9

**UNITED STATES:**
E-mail: mk_dewitt@msn.com
Mail:    Box 463,
           Preston, WA 98050

$12  CAN / $10 USA (plus postage)
Other Countries - use CAN e-mail above

OR Order directly from 🎵 **GOSPEL FOLIO PRESS**
Webstore: www.gospelfolio.com
Toll Free Phone: 1-800-952-2382  E-mail: orders@gospelfolio.com

1955, first year in Trinidad;
first team-mate Helen Latham;
first home in Arima.

Why the big smile?
I was just accepted for
ministry in Trinidad.

Preston
Baptist, my
home church,
celebrates
its 100th
anniversary.

Meet the
family:
(left to right)
Earl, Marj,
June, Mom,
Roger, Dad,
Lois & yours
truly (mid
1950s).

Eager learners in my outdoor Bible study.

Our first of six church plants, a humble beginning.

1962, the year Donna Williamson and I "teamed up."

Edith and Donna among the poinsettia.

Furlough lets us relax at places like
Barkerville, gold-rush town in BC.

We enjoy Minter Gardens near Chilliwack.

I'm back
throwing
snowballs,
quite a
change!

Ruby loves her "brimmed hats."
(Chap.14).

Ridgewalk Camp and Conference Centre.

Cabins were built by local volunteers and help from Canada and the USA.

Ben Penner and I with our big catch.

Margaret Keeler, Ruby Thompson and I are prayer partners. (Dubbed "The 3 Musketeers").

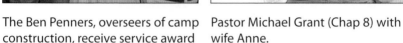

The Ben Penners, overseers of camp construction, receive service award from WT Dir., Albert Ehmann.

Pastor Michael Grant (Chap 8) with wife Anne.

Ben's memorial plaque at camp.

One-time fisherman guide, Tallboy, and his daughters (Chap. 13).

Marabella Church began in our front room.

Texaco bungalow.

Texaco bungalow
—Reassembled on church land.

Texaco bungalow
—First phase on the way up.

The real church is the people.

Teaching the young.

Pastor and Mrs Dietrich from Prince George, BC.

There is joy in serving Jesus.

Marabella's 40 Anniversary, reunion of the youth.

Max and I collaborating over the book.

My 80th birthday surprise, sisters Lois and Marj come to my Trinidad home for the first time.